INVESTING IN RENTAL PROPERTIES FOR BEGINNERS

BUY LOW, RENT HIGH

Let's Get Cash Flow IN!

By Lisa Phillips

ISBN-13: 978-1-7326445-0-2
ISBN-10: 1-7326445-0-0

Free Gift for My Readers

As a way of saying "Thank You" to my Readers I have a special gift for you. I'd like to give you access to this exclusive companion course which will help you supplement the information you've received from this book. These video trainings will help you pull together the rental properties at the lowest possible price and show you the exact CPR technique for finding rental properties! Click the link below and you'll have instant access to my Free Gift!

VISIT THIS SITE TO RECEIVE YOUR FREE GIFT
http://bit.ly/FreeGiftAndTraining

Table of Contents

Why I Wrote This Book

I am a working-class girl, with a working-class background who loves going back to her community and investing in real estate. But I wasn't always successful in real estate investing. Let me tell you the background story about how I went from being an unemployed engineer in foreclosure to earning $4,201 a month in rental income with a few fully paid off rental properties that cost less than $30,000.

I grew up poor but happy – you hear that a lot in the story of the United States. The same story of those who did not realize they were poor until they attended a charter high school in another part of town – talk about a wake-up call for both sides!

I start with this because I am proud of where I come from. I love my working-class roots. Everyone worked, and maybe they didn't make a ton of money, but you had all the necessities and a ton of other neighborhood kids to play with. It was fun, and a little wild, but you had hope that you could make it too. You have a culture of saying what's on your mind (which I didn't realize wasn't widespread until I went to a charter high school at a much higher socio-economic level, and realized NOT saying what was on your mind was more valued).

I can't emphasize enough how much I love my working-class roots; I love working-class people of all varieties, and millions here in America understand that background and story because it mirrors their own. But, life is a learning experience for a bright person who wants to climb the ladder of success, being inherently different than the new friends they make along the way. This is a book about understanding those differences, and being firm and proud of my background and culture (and wishing others to do the same)!

I attended school at the University of Nevada Las Vegas to be an electrical engineer. I worked hard, and I was proud of what I was able to accomplish. I didn't just sit around expecting anything to be handed to me. To support myself while I was in school, I did a lot of what I call the "side hustle." I would do anything – even things that were embarrassing. I've done mystery shopping. I also sold Cutco knives while I had an electrical engineering degree. I was so afraid of being insolvent that I would do whatever it took.

Eventually, my hard work and degree paid off – so I thought. I got a good job at IBM across the country from my family. I bought a nice house in Las Vegas at the top of the market. And then, in 2009, I was laid off, through no fault of my own. Actually, I was laid off twice. Not because of my work product – they hired me back because I was that good and that specialized at what I did. It was just a market downturn beyond my control. It was proof that you can be smart and follow everyone's advice, you can get a degree and look perfect on paper and still get laid off. That year, 2009, about 500,000 jobs *per month* were being lost in the U.S. I was putting out 20 or more job applications a day and not getting a bite. To make matters worse, the real estate market had tanked. I was stuck with no regular income, holding an overpriced home I couldn't sell for what I owed on it.

I ended up with a huge foreclosure on my credit report. It was really humiliating. This wasn't supposed to happen to smart, hard-working women like me. But there I was. I wanted to take that experience and survive it – I was handed lemons, and I was going to make the best lemonade you'd ever tasted.

Despite the foreclosure, I was determined to figure out how I could still invest in real estate and make money. That's how I stumbled on a system that allowed me to do it. It had to come out of my pain, but I did it. It wasn't fun being laid off and having my house taken by the bank, but I'm grateful for the lessons I learned as a result of that experience. Just like the pain of labor ends up giving you beautiful, precious babies, my pain in these struggles helped me give birth to a simple method of investing that leads to immediate cash flow.

Because of that horrible experience, I can now help you and anyone else out there who wants help. As of the writing of this book, I've helped over FIVE HUNDRED investors purchase their first investment property with happiness, love, and ease. I've personally coached over one hundred happy souls who are all making money and living their dreams. Yes, real estate investment can be that easy.

It took me a long time to determine the right markets. I made a ton of mistakes, and I learned from each of them. I know now how personally satisfying it is to go into lower income and working-class neighborhoods – like the one I grew up in – and giving hard-working folks a nice place to live at a reasonable price. I'm not looking to gentrify anything or push deserving people out of their homes. Over the years, I've learned how to do this right, and I've spent the last few years teaching other people how to achieve the same success I have achieved. All the while providing a valuable service to families who need a place to live.

This book outlines what I've learned about getting out of debt, finding the investment capital to begin, evaluating markets, investing in properties, and choosing the right tenants.

I pride myself in my ability to meet people where they are, personally and financially. I make sure that people know what kind of sacrifices they are going to have to make to get the ball rolling. I spend a lot of time talking to people to figure out what they actually want (which is different than what they think they should settle for) and then helping them build the investment portfolio of their dreams.

No matter how hopeless or helpless people may feel, there is hope, and there is help. You can get from where you are to where you want to be if you have the right information and the right guidance. You have choices. You can choose your path instead of trudging along on the one you find yourself on.

I've helped thousands of people create the world they want to live in (over 565 directly as coaching clients.) I take their hands and guide them to their ideal destinations. The information in this book is the first step on that journey.

Who Is This Book For?

Let me start by telling you who this book is *not* for. This book is not for the people who can call their parents and get an $80,000 loan just for asking. This is not for people who can just stroke a check and make things happen. This book is for regular, average people who want to know how they can find financial security through real estate investing.

Ask yourself these questions:

- Are you a new investor?

- Do you struggle to figure out how to obtain low-cost rental property?

- Are you frustrated by how difficult it is to determine if you are getting a good deal?

- Are you tired of buying tools, products, and training that are not tailored to your needs and your specific situation?

- Do you want to build a scalable real estate business that is automated, makes money, and lets you live a life of financial freedom?

- Are the only properties you see priced at $200,000 or more?

- Are you already an investor but you aren't receiving cash flow from your properties?

- Are the only houses you see located nowhere near you? Do you have to invest out of state, but have no idea where to start?

- Are you interested in purchasing a long-term, stable rental property investment?

If you answered "yes" to any of these questions, ***this book is for you.*** I will talk about my simple, step-by-step system for making at least $1,000 to $2,000 *per month per property* for a lifetime, with properties that only cost $30,000 to $50,000. You can do this in as little as 8 -12 weeks easily and effortlessly. We just have to see what's the right market for you, your budget, and where you're currently located.

This is the kind of investment property that helps with affordable housing. It can give you a long-term tenant base – it isn't unusual to have the same tenant for twenty years or more. We're making money, and they're getting a decent place to stay. This is an investment strategy that can bring long-term growth *and* stability for families who deserve it. This type of housing is the last line of defense for a lot of people.

We can be socially responsible with what we are doing. I need you to be on board with this concept before you go any further with this book. Television shows have glamorized flipping houses, but when you are doing anything but renovation that gets these houses ready for a modest family, you are part of the squeeze that everyone is feeling at every level, especially people at working class levels.

This book is not for people who are interested in flipping and gentrifying neighborhoods. This book is for people who are interested in making money in a way that gives back to the people who are the backbone of our communities, the hardworking folks who do the difficult work and just want a decent place to live and a safe place for their children to grow up and play. This book is for people who can't go to the Bank of Mom and Pop and get a

$50,000-$80,000 loan for a down payment on a $250,000-$400,000 house.

This book is for people like you and me.

CHAPTER 1

Why Invest in the Sub-30-$50K Market?

I spend a lot of time talking to people who want to invest in real estate but are intimidated by the high prices associated with purchasing homes. After all, most of us don't have hundreds of thousands – or even tens of thousands – laying around with which we can buy a house.

You've probably heard the old saying – it takes money to make money. That's true to a degree. But it doesn't take nearly as much as you might think. I will let you in on a little secret – you don't need to spend six figures or more on a house if you know what to look for.

I talk about real estate investing *every single day.* I've made mistakes and watched others make mistakes. I've coached people through those mistakes and learned a lot in the process. That kind of constant immersion has allowed me to get better at my craft – just as you will if you follow my system.

The first three houses I bought were purchased for $13,000; $25,000; and $35,000 respectively. I then purchased a fourth for $11,000. I was able to make $1,900 a month *positive cash flow* from the first three rental houses, which gave me plenty of money to do the renovations necessary on the fourth house without dipping into my own pocket. The financial independence that this real estate investing strategy has brought me is not only attainable but can literally be the easiest path to consistent monthly income.

These homes aren't found in gated communities. They are found in working-class neighborhoods. That doesn't mean that they can't be decent houses in decent neighborhoods. I'm not a slumlord. I've figured out how to use information that is freely available on the internet to view and analyze these neighborhoods. Google Maps "street view" is an excellent resource for looking at what you could buy without even getting out of your chair. We'll talk more about it later – but you can tell a lot just from the front yard of a house.

This is the gift I'm giving you. After I'm done with you, you will have the skills to *KILL* it in this industry using affordable homes that everyone else is snubbing their noses at.

After reading this book, you will have an outline of how the strategy works. Then you can decide if you want to delve deeper into the resources I'll reference at the end. You can see for yourself how easy it will be to jump in and build your real estate investing business your way.

This reminds me of a story of a lady named Isabel who lived in New Jersey. Isabel had saved $100,000. (Now, you DON'T need 100k. I work with people who have as little as 10k-15k saved up to start their portfolio – this is just to illustrate even if you have a significant life savings, you can still get horrible advice.) Isabel went to a real estate investment company in New York where she was told her "best" strategy was to invest her entire 100k (life savings) into a condo in New York City where she would net $300 a month after expenses. She thought that didn't make sense, and asked why she would do that. They looked at her with a straight face and said, "Because it will appreciate!"

And THAT'S why I wrote this book. Let me explain. That wasn't necessarily bad advice. If you have $500,000 in the stock market, then yes, put that 100k in a condo (that's old, requires maintenance, and has way too tenant-friendly laws), and in 10-20 years – yes! It WILL appreciate.

However, for the average person without half a million dollars in the stock market, that's not a good idea at all. But they weren't going to tell Isabel that because they were used to high net worth individuals. That they dealt with people who have one to five million dollars. They were going to take her money and leave her in a very vulnerable position – for $300 a month.

Isabel called me a couple of months ago to thank me. After working together, she purchased two properties in a New Jersey town that everyone thought was horrible for $35,000 each. She earns $2200 a month in revenue, and her husband now wants to buy another, and he believes Isabel is the smartest woman on earth. THAT'S the best strategy for someone who has a little bit of cash.

The reason I tell that story is for you to understand that the messenger matters. If the only route to real estate investing and passive income is by having half a million dollars, their advice is inappropriate if you bring in 70k a year. If their advice relies on them asking their parents for an $80,000 loan, and that's nowhere in your future, then their advice is not for you.

The messenger matters. And if the person who invests in real estate had to do it within their means, with no loans, and knew they only could rely on themselves, their advice, strategies, and methods are going to be tailored to that reality. It's how the 99% successfully invest. Make sure you learn from those who can relate to you and understand where you are coming from financially and resource wise.

CHAPTER 2

Using the CPR Technique

The *CPR Technique* is what I call the method I've developed to be successful in the real estate business. We will go over it in depth in Chapter 4, **"How the CPR Technique Works,"** but for now I need to explain how all the real estate investing advice you've been fed over the years has been overly complicated and hasn't served anyone but the wealthy.

My strategies work anywhere and everywhere. Not just in my part of the world – the D.C. area – but in your area as well. And not only in the United States. Using the power of the internet, you can apply this technique in Canada, France, or the U.K. Where there are people, there are houses, and where there are houses, there are people who need to live in them. I've helped over 200 investors do this all over the United States (the majority have been in New York, DC, Atlanta, Florida, Texas, and California). This systematic blueprint demonstrates how to find and analyze Working Class Neighborhoods (WCNs) and rental properties using the power of the internet. You can utilize this technique for FREE.

What's great about it is that it can be profitable from the get-go. Not all properties are profitable – not even all properties in this discounted price range. This technique is designed to ferret out the profitable ones from the money pits.

Of course, it is your choice. You don't have to use what you will learn in this book. If you don't use it, however, you run the risk of wasting your time and throwing money away. Be smart, be efficient, and increase your cash flow. Isn't that what you'd rather do?

This CPR Technique has worked for me personally in Ohio, Maryland, and Virginia. It's the same wherever I go. It has also worked for my clients all over North America. It's a method. It's systematic. Don't forget – I have an engineering degree. I understand math and formulae and how to make equations balance the way I want them to. Never fear – you don't need to be an engineer to understand this method any more than you need to understand the engineering that goes into designing a smartphone. You only need trust that the engineers designed the phone's operating system the right way. Then you can use it the way you want. Likewise, you can trust that I designed this real estate investment system the right way, and all you have to do is use it!

For example, I worked with a brother and sister team, Kim and Chuck[1], who wanted to get into real estate investing. They used my technique to buy a triplex in D.C. for $75,000. If you know anything about D.C., you know that the median home price there is about $500,000[2]. They were able to get $1,200 a month for one unit, and $1,230 for the other – that's $2,430 a month coming in!

---

[1] Names and certain identifying details here and throughout this book have been changed to maintain the privacy of my clients. Some stories are compilations, but all are based on real clients' experiences. I can't promise you that your experience will be exactly the same as theirs, but I can say that I haven't seen it fail yet if you follow these steps.

[2] https://www.zillow.com/washington-dc/home-values/

These are real people who quickly found themselves with cash flow that they could use.

By the time you are done reading this book, you should be able to search for, analyze, and purchase outstanding real estate investment properties at rock bottom prices. I will also show you how to achieve worry-free property management. I had one client, Mike, who wanted to invest in properties, but who recognized that his time was money. He didn't want to have to run out to the property every time a lightbulb or pilot light went out. I taught him how to utilize worry-free management techniques and pair them with high cash flow income. All of this was within a small radius of where he lived using free online tools and the roadmap I gave him.

The trick to all of this is *leverage*. Leverage can mean a few different things, all of which you can use to your advantage. Economically, it means using borrowed money to increase your ultimate income. It can also mean the exertion of influence over a situation, person, or event, to achieve your desired outcome. Famed investor Robert Kiyosaki said, *"Leverage is the reason some people become rich and others do not become rich."* The key to beating everyone at this game is methodically and systematically leveraging FREE resources. My electrical engineering training has definitely come into play in creating these solid metrics.

It may sound complicated, but it isn't. This is just completely practical advice gleaned from experience and knowledge of how working-class neighborhoods operate. It comes from my experience living in these neighborhoods, and my time investing in them. There is no need to pay companies like RealtyTrac or RentFax for a neighborhood analysis.

WHY SHOULD YOU LISTEN TO ME?

There are a lot of people out there who will give you advice about how to invest in real estate. Why should you believe me over anyone else? Well, let me tell you where I came from and how I got where I am. You will see that this isn't just theory or something I learned out of a book. I came through it myself, and I'm leading by example.

I wasn't born with wealth – I earned every penny of what I have myself. I believe that I have a duty to help as many people as possible get to where I've gotten. If I can, you can. "Everyone to whom much is given, of him much will be required.[3]" I know I've been given a lot – this is how I make good on that gift.

I've helped hundreds of people directly, and I'm still doing it every day, changing lives. It is so meaningful when someone reaches out to thank me for helping them achieve their dreams. They didn't think it was possible, but I gave them the system to make it a reality.

When I was young, I was told the same thing most people were told: That the path to success was a straight line from school to a good job on my mom's side, and a southern father who always promoted that you didn't need schooling but could join the army, be a mechanic or plumber. Both methods really promote working for other businesses versus creating your own. Study hard, work hard, play the traditional game, and you will succeed. So that's what I did (remember, I was taught all roads lead to getting a "good job"). I graduated college with a degree in electrical engineering. That degree led to the job I thought I wanted with

---

[3] Luke 12:48

IBM. I moved across the country for that job, and with the promise of a steady paycheck from a blue-chip company, I bought an extremely overpriced house in Las Vegas. Of course, that's not what I *thought* I was doing, but that's what happened because I didn't really know *what* I was doing. For a little while, it worked just fine.

I was proud of myself. I set a goal – a good education, and a good job with a nice house in a great neighborhood – and I achieved it. I thought I had made it. I did what my parents and teachers told me to do. I assumed I was set for life.

But of course, I wasn't.

As often happens, the unexpected occurred. The economy took a sharp downturn, and I was laid off not once, but twice. I didn't do anything wrong to be fired, it was just simple downsizing due to economic constraints. I had no seniority with IBM, and I was the first to go. They took me back, and then let me go again. If you were alive in 2009, you probably remember how many jobs were lost at that time.

I finally realized that I could no longer afford my mortgage. I was facing the ultimate humiliation – foreclosure. The house I had worked so hard for was going to be taken back by the bank.

Following the prescribed path – being the 'good girl' and playing by all the traditional rules – was clearly not going to work for me. I had to step off the path I was on and start thinking outside of the box if I was going to turn this situation around. So, for the first time in my life, I did the exact opposite of what the so-called 'experts' would have advised me to do and what anyone would have expected me to do – I bought a house. Yup, when my finances were going south, when I had no money and no prospects, I *bought* a house.

It was a condo, to be exact. Instead of spending hundreds of thousands as I did on my Las Vegas house, I spent $35,000 on a house in a working-class neighborhood in Ohio. For that price, you'd expect a falling down house in a crime-ridden neighborhood. But that wasn't the case. It was a decent neighborhood. The house wasn't fancy, but it was nice. I eventually found a job in D.C., and was able to easily rent the house when I relocated. The rental income provided me with a small amount of monthly cash flow.

I was inspired. With just a little bit of research and daring, I found a property that kept me from being homeless, jobless, hungry and broke. I realized on a fundamental and visceral level that I could live well and earn money without having a traditional job if I owned and invested in real estate. I saw first-hand how easy and affordable it was to purchase lower-priced properties.

I was hooked!

I lived this way for about six months. I developed and used the CPR Technique I will describe in more detail later. Lo and behold, I was able to repeat this success in the D.C. area, in Baltimore, Maryland, and Richmond, Virginia. On my weekends! This was doable everywhere. I could find properties in wonderful and safe neighborhoods, full of great working-class people who were mostly hourly and uniformed workers. I didn't need to help provide housing for white collared, salaried workers. They could do for themselves. Instead, I could help the working class who needed the help.

My vision was set. I knew what I wanted to do, and how to do it. I wanted to show others the systems I had learned. I started a YouTube channel. At first, only a few people watched my videos. Slowly but surely, though, more viewers rolled in. Soon enough I was contacted by someone who offered to pay me to work one-on-one with her to teach her the details of my system. She said she didn't know anyone else doing this system to ask for help, but knew that this was the way she could get started in real estate investing.

I accepted her offer, and we worked together to map out a plan. It was fun, exciting, and revealed that this system could work everywhere, for everyone. Guess what? You shouldn't be surprised – it worked for her. In total, she spent $63,000 for a duplex and the renovations it needed, and now she collects $1,400 a month in rent for it.

The moral of the story is this: if I can do it, and if my clients can all do it, *you can do it, too!*

SO MANY LIVES HAVE BEEN CHANGED. AND WE'RE ALL BLESSED BECAUSE OF IT.

My client, Darlene N., watched my videos and participated in some of my group calls. She learned not only from me but from the other people on the calls and in my exclusive Facebook group. She soon bought her first property – a two-bedroom, two and a half bath townhome in the Orlando, FL area – for $25,000. It needed only $5,000 in repairs. Her total investment of only $30,000 now gets her $800 a month in rent!

Darlene was scared at first. Orlando was a hot market at the time she was investing, and she was competing with investors from all over the state and country. This created some additional challenges, but it was not impossible. She persisted, and she found the perfect property for her to invest in.

If Darlene can do it, you can do it, too!

To meet Darlene, make sure you sign up to join the Sub30k Mastermind Group (It's free!)

Facebook.com/groups/Sub30kMastermindGroup

CHAPTER 3

How I Make $975 a Month from a $13,000 House

The five steps to finding a lucrative, yet affordable rental property are:

1. Find the right market

2. Find the right price

3. Find the right team to work with

4. Have the right tenants

5. Invest in yourself through mentoring

Each of these steps is crucial – if you are missing any of them, you are not following the system. We will go over them each in turn below.

Step One: Find the Right Market

There is no one right market. They exist all over the country and all over the world. The right market is a highly-targeted niche market that is full of high-quality homes that need little renovation. Also, what is the right market for one person, might not be the right market for another. So much of how you build your rental property portfolio should be personal, and not just regurgitating cookie-cutter advice.

Of course, part of understanding what the right market is, is understanding what the *wrong* market is.

The wrong market is in overpriced cities like New York, San Francisco, and Austin. Markets that are exceptionally tenant friendly are also difficult. Cities like New York, where rent control and the existence of laws that make it difficult to evict a tenant who doesn't pay rent on time, are havens for 'professional' tenants that are hard to get rid of.

Other things to look for to determine if you are looking at the 'wrong' market are:

- Jobs leaving the area

- Cheap properties, but only in neighborhoods with high crime rates

- Extremely low rents

- Houses that are in extreme disrepair

If these conditions exist, you are in the wrong market, with the wrong inventory and selection. The financial payoff is very low and you won't be able to get the cash flow required to gain real financial independence. Expensive home renovations mean that the costs are too high for the property to be cost-effective to own as an investment. The income generated will be too low to offer you financial freedom. Crime in the neighborhood – or, the wrong kind of crime, like we'll talk about later – will keep away stable, long-term renters. Remember, we want 20-30 years of stable income – it's not hard, but you have to know how to be just a little bit discerning.

So now that we know what the wrong market is, what are the things you want to look for to see what the right market is?

In the right market, you'll find a massive inventory with which you can easily build your portfolio. It won't be overly competitive. Competition, after all, drives up prices, and we're looking to buy low. The more supply, the less the demand, and the fewer bidding wars for the same property. In the right market, rents are relatively high compared to the price of the property. The neighborhoods are safe with low crime rates. These neighborhoods are full of ordinary, hard-working people who pay their bills on time every month. These properties can run for years without having problems, and the tenants stay to raise kids – that can be 30+ years with a stable, long-term tenant. Passive income like clockwork for a long time.

When you find these houses in the right market, you can get an affordable start to investing in the real estate market. With costs this low, it is relatively easy to get the funding and financing. They are easy to launch and scale.

There are *thousands* of these markets to try – but you only need to find one. I guarantee you there is one near where you are right now if you know how to look.

Remember, it has to be the right market for YOU, with an emphasis on Y-O-U. Some people are more comfortable in urban areas, and some people are more comfortable in rural areas. There's no right or wrong; there's only your comfort zone.

How far you are willing to travel is another issue. If you need to travel out of state, can you drive to where you need to go? How expensive are plane tickets? Is there a similar market that is cheaper to fly to? Do you have family or friends in the area who will let you stay with them when you go, or will you pay a hotel expense? If you do pay for travel and hotels, how much does it cost in one location versus the other? There is a lot to consider than just the property. You should list all of these factors side by side and make sure include these in your calculations.

Step Two: The Right Price

Real estate prices can vary in different parts of the country. Urban areas tend to be more costly than rural areas, and growing cities tend to be more expensive than ones on the decline. So how do you know if the property you are looking at is the right price?

You'll know it is the wrong price if you find that your estimated cash flow will be less than $200 a month. You may be told that 'appreciation' is the reason for the high cost – that's a red flag as well. Some other signs that you are not looking at a house at the right price are:

- It takes twenty-five or more years to have a cash flow of $800 – $2,200

- It takes up too much of your debt-to-income ratio[4]

- You won't be able to handle the costs associated with the house if it is vacant for a period of time

---

[4] Your debt-to-income ratio is the amount of debt you have as compared to the amount of income you have. It is calculated as a fraction or percentage, and that number is what banks use to decide where or not to extend credit to you. Generally, you want to keep it less than 1/3 or 33%.

- The financial payoff is very low

- To purchase the home, you have to over-leverage your other assets, which limits your ability to fund future endeavors

- You don't have much wiggle room to handle the normal ups and downs that happen

- The income generated from the property is too low

- It will take too much time to recover the costs of your investment

So, now that we know how to recognize the *wrong* price, how do we know how to recognize the *right* price?

The right price is one where you can *easily* cover the carrying costs in the event of a temporary vacancy. You would still get significant tax benefits, and the total time to complete cash flow (paying off the mortgage and keeping all the rent for yourself) is only three to five years.

The reasons why this is the formula for the 'right price' is because it allows you to get a cash flow that grows quickly over time. You can build a large portfolio quickly in a way that is easy to acquire and fund. You won't over leverage yourself. In this way, you can assure yourself safety and security. Isn't that what you want for yourself? I know it is what I crave.

I had a client that only liked Polish, working-class neighborhoods – the kind in which she grew up. And that's OKAY.

Sure, that neighborhood had homes that were more expensive (55k-70k), and slightly lower cash flow – but she was happy to build that, and it was still cheaper than what mainstream advice suggested. It's okay if SUB30k actually means 60k for you – because that's your comfort level. So, follow YOUR instincts, and do what you feel good about – and don't always chase the cheap dollars if you're not comfortable with it. You have to live with it, not the person who gave you the advice. And it's NOT always about money. It's always a fine line of discerning how inexpensive an investment is weighed against how we envisioned our investment portfolio to shape up.

Step Three: The Right Team

Before you even choose a market, ALWAYS verify that it's the right market, with the right TEAM! And, you should have this verified before you PURCHASE your first investment. I'll show you what I mean in Chapter 9 "Investing Out of State."

I am NOT a landlord – I am a rental property owner who has chosen the right investment and infrastructure around it to receive passive income and financial freedom. I am NOT a landlord. I take calls from my property management company only, not tenants. I do not call contractors for repairs, as that's not my job – my team handles that. So, if you want true financial freedom, finding a market that already has the right team in place is critical to creating a business and not another job.

Like most things, you are not going to be able to do this entirely on your own. You will need to assemble a team to help you through some of the steps of this process. You may need a real estate agent, a plumber, an electrician, a general handyman, a painter, lawn care service provider, a banker, a home inspector, and any number of other professionals. Some of these people or businesses will be great, and others will just take your money and do a substandard job. Others may foul things up in a way that costs you more money in the end. That's why it is so essential to assemble the right team.

The wrong team won't come with any references. There's nothing wrong with finding someone out of the phone book or through a Google search if you get independent references.

References (online reviews are JUST as valid as seeing photos on the contractor's phone) will tell you how trustworthy or competent this person is. Did tools, appliances, or other equipment go missing? Did they bump the walls or scratch the floors during the process? Did they show up when they were supposed to and finish the job by the date promised? Were there hidden costs? There are specific questions you should ask the references – it isn't enough to just get a written reference. It could be a family member or friends that wrote the references.

The wrong team won't 'get' you the results you want. You know what I mean by this – how many times in your life have you tried to explain something to someone, and they just look at you with that blank stare? Or maybe they smile and nod and then speak as if they haven't heard a word you said. It's a great feeling when someone gets where you are coming from. That's worth waiting for.

As much as I love a good bargain, I've learned over the years that you get what you pay for, especially when it comes to your team. Beware of super-cheap providers you find on Craigslist or other sites. You might find a good contractor looking for a side hustle or just starting out, or, more likely, you will find someone who can't get business any other way.

If you find yourself with the wrong team, you run the risk of losing money during renovation as the costs skyrocket. You need to know on the front end if the people you hire are going to finish their job well, with integrity, and with the care and awareness that their reputations are at stake.

Time really is money. If the people you hire take six weeks to do a two-week job, then you miss out on four weeks of rent. With a rental business, you need a quick turnaround. Missing a month or two of rent unnecessarily can be the difference between being profitable and losing money in the short term.

Real estate investing really is a location game. You need a team that is familiar with the particular market in which you are investing – you don't put granite countertops and copper pipes in a $25,000 home in a working-class neighborhood, for example. No one living in these neighborhoods needs, wants, or expects complicated wainscoting or fancy cabinetry. You need location-specific information to make sure that your property fits within the aesthetic and expectations of the neighborhood in which you are investing.

The right team is reliable and experienced and has several contacts that you can use to expand your team. They are familiar not only with the market itself but with you. They take the time to get to know you and your particular wants and needs. It's also essential that they understand the laws governing your rental in that location. Wouldn't it be awful for an agent to sell you a house that is not zoned for the type of rental you want to do? Or for an electrician to do work that didn't comply with the codes in the area?

The whole idea of this type of investment is *passive income.* Passive income means that once it is set up, you don't have to do much but own it – your team takes care of the day-to-day details. This can only happen with a trustworthy team. When you know they are going to do right by you, then you can rest peacefully and easily, knowing that your investment is working for you and not against you.

You can learn a lot from the right people. A good real estate agent can teach you a lot about the neighborhood you are considering. A good handyman may be able to suggest other materials or ideas for your home which will last longer or save you money. You can't be an expert in everything, but you can learn from the experts you hire. They can help you fill in any knowledge gaps you might have when entering a new market.

In any given market, there are hundreds of professionals to choose from. You only need a few to get your real estate business running on autopilot – the only trick is to make sure that those few are the *right* few.

You might think it is putting the cart before the horse, but make sure you get that team in place before you make your purchase. In fact, get that team in place before you even settle on the market. You won't be able to successfully invest in a market if you can't build the team, so it makes sense to build the team first so that you know you will have the right people to rely on once things get cranking. Choose the market based on the support structure; don't find the support structure after you've chosen the market. You can't. It might not be there.

Step Four: The Right Tenants

Having the right tenants in your property can make the difference between having smooth, passive income and having a massive headache and constant stress. So how do you make sure you have the right tenants?

It's important to have a thorough application process that will screen out the wrong tenants. However, it needs to be appropriate for THAT neighborhood. Don't expect someone who makes a decent income, but is not a high net worth individual (i.e., earns 70k a year – and yes, for many that IS high net worth) to not have a credit blemish in these neighborhoods. However, you shouldn't allow anyone with multiple "charge-offs" of non-paying credit accounts in either. You can accept people with evictions and multiple charge-offs, but discerning investors know how to circumvent their risks by collecting more up front for the security deposit (first and last month's rent, two to three months of security deposits). That's the art of learning how to invest in these neighborhoods. Here are some things to look for:

The wrong tenants are ones who don't earn the minimum amount necessary to pay the rent each month. They also don't have a very good track record at meeting their regular obligations. Running a credit report will give you this information. Potential tenants who have court records – not just criminal records, but civil records as well indicate that they are not the type of responsible people you want to have in your rental property. We'll talk more about the specifics of the screening process later.

The idea that tenants should have "first and last month's rent" is a cliché for a reason. If they don't have enough money to put down a deposit, whether you call it a security deposit to cover potential damages or "last month's rent," they aren't likely going to meet their obligations down the road. Things happen – cars break down and need repair; people get hurt or become ill and need to take off work, potentially decreasing their income; or they get a traffic ticket that they must pay. While these things can be tragic for the people involved, they can also mean that you aren't going to get the money you are owed for providing them a decent place to live. People who can't come up with a deposit are usually people who haven't planned for emergencies or even foreseeable contingencies.

The last thing you want is for your monthly rental income to become unreliable. After all, the reason why you started this whole thing was to create regular income. You don't want to have to involve the Court system to resolve disputes. Courts don't move as quickly as you might like, and they can be expensive and inconvenient to utilize. Often it is more cost-efficient to cut your losses and not even bother, as the time and expense of Court involvement is more than what you'd gain if you win your case. Now, don't hesitate to use the courts as needed, but the point I am trying to make is to be discerning enough so that you don't have to go to that level in the first place. It's absolutely doable.

Of course, there are bad tenants. I'm here to teach you how EASY it is to avoid them if you know what the heck you're doing. And we do.

The right tenant, on the other hand, is someone who can be a reliable, long-term tenant. You want to look for someone who has a documentable habit of meeting his or her obligations, a consistent employment history, and an appreciation for *your* property. One to two blemishes are normal and acceptable – but more than that requires you collect additional financial reserves up front. Ideally, this is not just a place for them to lay their head at night and store all their junk – this is their home for the time being, and they should take as much pride in it as you do.

When you have the right tenant, you won't have to worry about bothering with the legal system, either calling the police because of illegal activity (or having the police called by neighbors or others) or engaging the Magistrate or other civil courts to handle eviction or proceedings to be reimbursed for expensive damages.

The right tenant can give you peace of mind. Not just emotionally, but financially. You can have a steady stream of reliable income, year after year. No extra time or effort is needed to run your business. You can spend your time doing what is needed to improve or expand on your business, not manage the headaches that go along with a bad tenant.

There are so many reasons that getting the right tenant is an important part of the system I've devised. You just need to know how to find them in your particular market. Each market is different, and you will have to use different criteria to evaluate them. Figuring out what that criteria should be is the trick. But don't worry – you can find the right tenants anywhere. If you follow these steps, you can find quality tenants in your rental, wherever it is, and receive rental income.

Remember Kim and Chuck, the brother and sister team I talked about in Chapter Two? Remember how they found a triplex in D.C. for $75,000 – that's only $25,000 per unit. They were fortunate that the house came with two good tenants who were paying $1,100 per month *each*. It didn't take long before they were able to find the right tenants for the third unit who is paying $1,300. That means that Kim and Chuck are getting $3,500 per month on a house they only paid $75,000 for. That's what the right tenants did for Kim and Chuck, and what they can do for you.

Step Five: Invest in Mentoring

When building a successful real estate business, you can go about it two different ways:

1. You can figure it out all by yourself and waste a ton of money and time by making mistakes on your own. Or,

2. You can get help from someone who has already made the mistakes and learned from them. Someone who has already paid the price can fast track you on to the road to success.

Of course, it is important to find a mentor you trust. Do your research, and talk to other people who have used that mentor to make sure you are getting what you need from that person. I'm never offended when people want to know about my qualifications and successes with mentoring. Asking those questions is just part of the due diligence you should be doing.

It's important to find the right mentor. The right mentor is someone who, like me, is willing to meet you where you are. There are no one size fits all solutions to every problem. Your individual needs, goals, and desires are different from anyone else's. Make sure your mentor recognizes that and doesn't try to make you a clone of themselves. Your investment portfolio should be as unique to you as your fingerprints. We learn best by being in the energy and presence of those who have experience in a field, and this is no different.

When you find the right mentor and engage their services, you will get a number of benefits such as:

Return on Investment. Think of what you pay your mentor as 'tuition.' You wouldn't expect to be a doctor or lawyer without going to medical school or law school. And, despite the high costs of medical school and law school, wannabe doctors and lawyers go to those schools because they know they will ultimately gain way more than what they pay. It's the same with mentoring – you have to pay in advance for the knowledge you need in order to be an expert. And when you do, you will find that you get paid back in multiples. You will get into the market faster and more strategically, you will make fewer mistakes, and overall you will have quicker acquisition of property and conversion to rental income. Mentoring pays for itself and then some. And you'll leave saying "Investing in real estate is EASY!" Trust me, this isn't everyone's story, but it can be your story.

Leverage. You can leverage your mentor's experience for your advantage. Wouldn't it be great to stand on someone's shoulders to reach the top instead of climbing all the way from the bottom by yourself as I did?

Accountability. Doubts often creep in at night and affect your ability to function during the day. It's easy to ignore what isn't right in front of you. The distractions of everyday life can make getting things done difficult. A good mentor will hold you accountable to your goals. You will set deadlines and your mentor will make sure you meet them. If no one is looking over your shoulder, would you really get it done?

Access. A good mentor can open doors for you. You will have access to their contacts, knowledge, and resources. They can give you good intel on the ground, and the phone number of a reliable contractor.

Focus. A mentor can keep you focused. On your own, you might play the "what if" game to your detriment – what if I do it this way? Or that way? Or these things, too? A mentor can help you keep your eyes on the prize. In this case, the prize is a low-cost property between 30 and 50 thousand dollars that gives you immediate cash flow. One single focus, one single intent.

SUMMARY

It seems simple when you spell it out like that, doesn't it? The five steps to get your real estate business going with a steady cash flow to keep you financially safe and secure are:

1. The right market
2. The right price
3. The right team
4. The right tenants
5. The right mentor

This is all it takes to have *The Right Stuff* in your real estate business. So, what are you waiting for?

RHONDA J.'S STORY OF FAILURE AND TRIUMPH

Rhonda J. already had one investment property when she met me and signed up for me to be her mentor. She was a hard-working woman with many irons in the fire – she worked as a bookkeeper and a government contractor. She saw one of her bookkeeping clients, a contractor, making money on his real estate investments and she wanted to do the same. She spent a long time looking – because she didn't know my simple, straightforward system – before finding a property in which to invest. The house she found and ultimately bought was a great house with good bones, but it was in a neighborhood that had too much crime. It was difficult for her to find a decent, reliable tenant who was willing to live in that neighborhood. She had to keep dropping the rent until she found someone which delayed and decreased her cash flow – precisely the opposite of what she wanted!

After I started working with her, she was able to quickly find another house only ten minutes away from the first. It was not far in terms of distance, but the neighborhood was worlds better, and she was able to make a profit much more quickly. She asked a lot of intelligent questions that helped her narrow her focus and find what she wanted. Rhonda was also an active participant in the weekly group meetings. She found that she learned just as much from the other people who were on a similar journey. She didn't just get information from the group either; she got emotional support from a collection of people who had the same fears and apprehensions. Now, instead of being afraid, she's eager to get her next property!

CHAPTER 4

How the CPR Technique Works

The CPR Technique that I have developed involves getting data from three critical metrics. Just like you can't skip any of the five steps I outlined in the previous chapter, you can't skip any of these metrics if you want an affordable house with minimal maintenance in a decent neighborhood. These three metrics are:

1. Crime

2. Photos

3. Rents

I call them the "CPR Metrics," and they are the backbone of the CPR technique. Just like CPR[5] can save your life, CPR Metrics can save the metaphorical life of your real estate business as well as your pocketbook – because you shouldn't buy just any "cheap" house you find!

I've found ways to streamline the data collection using the internet as a screening device. Of course, nothing compares to seeing it in person, but you can weed out a lot of undesirable properties using this technique. This helps you avoid wasting time visiting properties that aren't going to work.

---

[5] Cardiopulmonary Resuscitation

To get the information I need, I search for real estate online, focusing on the three crucial criteria:

1. Searching for the available crime reports *find out how to access MLS*
2. Viewing photos on the MLS[6] listing
3. Noting the average rents for the address/neighborhood

You have probably heard that when you look for a house, you should look at the schools in the area. The quality of the schools can be a good indicator of the quality of the neighborhood. While this may be true for more upscale neighborhoods, it isn't the case for working-class neighborhoods. In these neighborhoods, families are looking for safe, clean places to live and may not have the luxury of being highly selective about schools with a higher number of Advanced Placement classes or extra-curricular activities. It is a different beast. The better you know what skills you need to find these properties, the more successful your search will be. I've had many investors I've helped after they came to a dead end tell me, "The schools were ranked low, so I wasn't sure!" Well, schools shouldn't be the main criteria in this demographic. This is one of those skills where you have to know what makes a difference, and what doesn't. And in this case, the crime statistics are 1000x more important than the school ranking. In a working-class neighborhood, the key metrics are crime and rent, not school choice. This doesn't mean parents don't care about the schools, but spending exponentially more for housing to be in a high-ranked school district isn't an available option, so the school that is close is the school that will do. And trust me,

---

[6] MLS stands for "Multiple Listing Service" and it is a warehouse, of sorts, of homes for sale. Real Estate Agents and Brokers will list the houses they have for sale through MLS in order to cast a broader net for potential buyers.

that's fine (every school has a path for those more academically gifted to go to honors/advanced placements).

Let's look at an example of how I use this technique to find homes to buy. I need to know if a particular house is one I want to invest in. There is a lot of information on the internet. Some of it is good, and some of it is useless and trash. I have figured out over the years how to take in the key, important factors that really determine a person's perception and comfort level, and disregard the rest. This may seem like common sense, but it has come from years of experience in several different states. It's a valuable method for diagnosing an investment using sound techniques.

First, I go to a site like Realtor.com, Yahoo homes, Zillow, or Trulia. They each have different advantages. I tailor my search criteria for what I'm looking for: under $40,000 with three bedrooms and two bathrooms. Depending on where you are looking, you might not find any properties, or there may be a limited selection. If you are dead set on that particular area, you need to broaden your criteria – either raise the price or don't be so picky with the number of rooms. Generally, I'm willing to go an hour's drive from my focal point. The actual distance an hour's drive is will depend on where you are located. It could be 60 miles or, if you're in an area like D.C., it could only be ten miles because of traffic.

Once you have several hits on your search, look at the pictures. I like to sort my results by the number of pictures. The more pictures, the better! I keep a little notepad next to my computer where I can jot down details.

It's important to know what you're looking at. Some things which seem bad aren't, and some things which seem ok are actually pretty bad. For example, holes in the wall look terrible but are really easy and inexpensive to fix. I always look around the windows, ceilings, and the basement walls for signs of water damage because this can be a sign of major structural problems and can be very costly to repair. You can usually see water spots because it goes through the drywall. So, a large water spot on the wall may actually be much worse than a big, gaping hole in the wall. That gaping hold probably will cost you about $100 to fix.

Of all the things I can't stand when looking at properties, water damage is the big one. You have to go through more intensive inspections and clear things out when rehabilitating the property. With so many options on the market, why bother with these? Alternatively, you can use water damage as a negotiating point to get the price down even further. You might be able to get a house with water damage for next to nothing.

It's not always easy to tell from the pictures what you are seeing. What looks like water or other damage might just be dirt. With a practiced eye, though, you can do a pretty good job estimating common repair and other rehab costs for the property. That's one of my favorite parts about helping people, and I've developed materials and guides to help you train your eye to know what to look for. If you're interested in my advanced training in estimating common repairs costs (regardless of what state you're located), you can purchase it for $7 at http://www.affordablerealestateinvestments.com/common-repair-costs-and-estimates-for-renovations. The training is only available at this price to those who purchase the book. Otherwise, the only way to see this training is to stay until month four of my *Investing Made Easy Monthly Membership*, which currently runs $37.97/month)

For example, my client, Yolanda, bought a house with a bathroom that looked like it hadn't been cleaned in years. It was truly disgusting. Most people would have just replaced the tub and fixtures if they even bothered with it at all. Not Yolanda – she knew she was just looking at dirt and wasn't afraid of hard work. She spent two weeks of elbow grease and less than a hundred dollars in cleaning products and ended up with a sparkling, like-new bathroom anyone would be proud of. She could have hired a maid service, but some jobs are small enough to do yourself (as long as you make sure it's sanitary and safe).

If the doors are not in good condition, that isn't a big concern. You can get a Home Depot or Lowe's credit card with no interest for several months, and replace a door – including installation! – for just $400-$500.

Plumbing can be a problem. To re-plumb a house in the Baltimore area costs around $3,000. I've done it piecemeal, and I've done it as one big project, and I've found that it is always cheaper to do the whole thing at once. PVC pipes are best – don't let anyone talk you into copper. It isn't necessary and is a theft risk. Criminals know that used PVC piping isn't worth anything, and it is easy (read: cheap!) to install. Copper, on the other hand, has a high resale value, and thieves will tear apart a house to get at it. What I am saying is, you can tell A LOT from the pictures alone.

Once you've found a house where the structure seems to be good, look up the crime reports. In some areas, you can go to the local police department's website and get that information. If that doesn't exist, other crime information websites exist that can help you. I've used www.CrimeReports.com, but I now prefer www.SpotCrime.com. I like to search for incidents in the past 30 days and have them mapped out. I'm visual, and it helps me to see where they are in relation to the house I'm looking at. It makes deciding on whether this is a viable candidate quick and efficient.

Remember: you're not looking for a neighborhood with NO crime. I'm not sure there IS such a thing as a neighborhood with no crime. I mean, just look at all these rich celebrities who live in exclusive, gated communities who are being accused of sexual crimes. You just need to know what you're looking at. I usually disregard the information about sex offenders, because it is generally out of date (some showed people who lived there ten years ago – those records are not well maintained, and you're looking at 20 years' worth of data with only a percentage of it being accurate today). If you are overly concerned, please go to the local sheriff's department and see if you can get more concrete and up-to-date information. Vehicle theft reports don't bother me. I go into super-posh neighborhoods in D.C., and they have the same rate of vehicle thefts. I'm ok with that for my personal comfort level. If there's a lot of theft, I might install burglar bars. They cost about $1,300, and you can make back that money within a couple of months while securing the building for a lifetime. No thief is going to bother trying to get through security bars on your property when the house next door doesn't have them. These are a great investment, especially if theft is an issue for the neighborhood. This makes your property very attractive to tenants who want to feel secure, and they will probably be willing to pay a little more in rent for that security. It's like, if you're running away from the bear, you only need to be faster than the slowest guy. It really is honestly that simple. So, not every crime should deter you from investing in a rental property.

I don't like assaults and physical crime. The more assaults I see, the less likely I am to buy a property. People should feel personally secure in their front yards. It's one thing if people's stuff gets taken; it is quite another if they feel personally insecure and there are numerous assaults ON THAT BLOCK.

I have found that in this subclass, it is definitely block to block. In my own experience, I had a home for five years that never once had the cops come to the street (I would check the reports every so often). However, just one block over – every few days there was a pretty serious physical assault. Crime is literally BLOCK TO BLOCK. I hope you really understand that.

[handwritten note: Can you build up a block]

You can also tell a lot from the yard and landscaping. They can tell you if the property and neighborhood are loved and cared for. Don't just look at the marketing photos, which can be staged. Look at the property on 'street view' of Google maps. And not just the property itself – look at the houses next door and across the street.

If it is a condo, the lawn should be manicured to show that the condo association is doing its job. If it is an independent house, look not only at the house itself but the neighbors' houses also.

Then, check out what properties are currently renting for in the neighborhood. You can look at a site like Padmapper.com, and it will give you a range. I like to estimate conservatively – figure you are going to get on the low end. Then, you will either get what you expect or more, but never less. Let's say that Padmapper.com says the range in this neighborhood is $600 to $1,000. It's a good bet you can get $750, especially since your home will be newly renovated and in good condition, which will put it light years ahead of a lot of other properties in the neighborhood (your competition). There are twelve months in a year, and you can count on having it rented eight of those twelve months. 8 x $750

= $6,000. Let's say you pay $19,000 for the house and then put in another $3,000 in repairs and renovations. That's $22,000 for the whole investment. The first year, you will make a 27% return. This is good because you are going to have this house the next year and the year after that and so on. This is only a rough estimate of the cash flow – we will go into more detail in Chapter 5 "Creative Financing" where we will analyze the cash flow.

My goal is to have a house for 15-20 years. So, when I do any repairs, I try to get a ten- to twenty-year warranty which makes the initial outlay of cash worth it in the long run. If the same thing breaks again in a few years, I can get it fixed again for nothing or at a reduced price. This makes everything cost efficient so if you lose your day job, you bought this at a low enough price and kept costs low enough that you can still collect a few hundred dollars a month (even if you're newly invested). Just a few years in, it's nearly all profit., Since I did any major repairs up front on the houses I do have, when something broke, it was minor. I generally pay about $400 a year in repairs, and every so often when part of the heating, ventilation, and air condition (HVAC) system needs repair it can reach up to $2000 – that's every six to ten years though.

These houses don't come to you in a neat package wrapped with a bow. You have to put a little work in them. Sometimes you have to put a little (or a lot of!) elbow grease in like Yolanda did. Roll up your sleeves and get in there and clean. It's amazing what cleaning can do to these houses. You can pay $400 for someone else to clean, or you can do it yourself, and the house can go from tragic to magic. I don't know why we get it in our heads that we can't do a little work and get our hands dirty. Get that out of your mind if you're dealing with me. Why not spend a few hours on a Saturday investing in a business that you can collect profits from for the next twenty years? I work smart, and you have to work smart if you want this to work for you. Be able to say, "I will do this or pay someone to do this, but I will GET IT DONE." Calling someone and making an appointment is not hard work. Just do it.

Once you have a list of houses selected as potential investment properties, call an agent and let them know the specific houses you want to view. If you say, "I want a $40,000 house," they will show you a $100,000 house. Be specific. Say, "I want to see the house at 123 Maple Dr., and the house at 428 Wormwood St." This might not be as easy as it sounds. A lot of agents don't want to deal with lower-priced properties because they aren't going to make tons of money off of the sale. That's where having the right team comes in. And, to assemble the right team, it is important to leverage your contacts – including your mentor – to get the right people on board. You need an agent who knows that she might not make a ton of money on this particular sale, but she will get repeat business from you and your referrals. You need to make that positioning clear from the very start, and that you need to SAY those things. You need an agent who understands that people without buckets of cash need to be able to buy homes too. Trust me; if you approach them without the right words, they will politely ignore your phone calls (I had a couple of agents do that). So, when I talk to an agent, I am assertive and say that "I need X and X, and that's it, and I plan on buying more" – that's it. Very straightforward and to the point. You need to say this or something like this, or be prepared to complain no one will take your call. Sometimes there is an art to this market and getting people on board, and that starts with positioning yourself as an authority right off the bat. *Be assertive*

Keep in mind that if you don't have these types of properties in your neighborhood or immediate city, that doesn't mean the whole thing is a no-go. You can find them in cities near you or even out of state. You don't have to be a local investor to make this work. If you don't know which neighborhoods to explore, ask your team!

There are two main reasons why I believe in this model:

1. It lowers the barrier for entry into real estate investing, especially for those who don't have a lot of money saved.

2. By purchasing a property at a low price point, you can assure yourself that you'll never be homeless. You'll always have a place to live. This kind of security is invaluable, especially for those who have faced the hardships of the real estate crash.

Remember: high photo count, low price, high rent, and low crime are all you need for a successful single-family buy and hold investment. You could use this approach directly, or tailor it to fit your own investment needs.

YOLANDA'S DREAM – DELAYED BUT MANIFESTED

Remember Yolanda? What I didn't tell you was that she had had a dream of real estate investing for ten years before she was able to pull the trigger all because of a common misconception. Yolanda believed what she was told – that she had to have money to make money, she needed perfect credit and a large down payment of $50,000 sitting in the bank to make one purchase. She thought without six figures lying around that real estate investing was just a pipe dream.

She saw her friends working hard for little gain – going from one job to another, being away from family and having little social life – just to stay afloat financially. She knew that wasn't for her, so she went looking and found my YouTube videos. After watching a few videos, she reached out, and I became her mentor.

She learned that not only could she invest without needing a huge amount in savings to start with, but she could do it with heart and purpose. Like me, Yolanda grew up in the kind of neighborhoods she's now investing in. I talked to her about her experience, and she said, "I do feel that when we go back to the neighborhoods and we tend to give the homes to someone to live in, we're not thinking like a landlord, and it's not only that we want the place rented. We go back in these apartments and houses and give a family a very nice home to enjoy – someplace they are proud to stay in and want to stay long term. You have tenants that will be tenants for years because they like the place so much because you've done a great job. You put a lot of work into making it a nice home. Then the community improves because families want to move into that kind of neighborhood and make the community better." So, they have a place that's affordable to stay long term where the price isn't going to shoot up, and you have a business partner that pays the rent on time 99% of the time and enjoys living there. It is a mutually beneficial relationship, and a human relationship – you are providing a reliable long-term rental to a deserving family who appreciates it.

Imagine that! Doing a good deed and achieving financial security at the same time! Witnessing success like Yolanda's is why I do what I do. Spiritual finances and compassion can go hand in hand together!

Yolanda lived in New York, and we found the perfect market in Pennsylvania for her to invest in. She is now on house number three and has even sent her friends and family my way, and they are doing it as well. She feels so financially free, and now she's able to focus on what her higher calling and purpose here is on earth. Ultimately, that's what I am empowering people to accomplish through real estate – free up some space for you to focus on your world impact. And it's working.

Please join the group of the kindest, most generous like-minded professionals making their investment dream a reality by joining the Sub30k Mastermind Group on Facebook: Facebook.com/groups/Sub30kMastermindGroup

CHAPTER 5

Creative Financing

When you don't have perfect credit and a large bank account, you can't just waltz into a bank and get a great loan on demand. Sometimes it takes a little creativity. I pride myself on my ability to look at someone's situation, seeing what they have at their disposal, and finding a way to make it work. Everyone can take a different path to investing in these modestly priced rentals; it just might not be a typical way.

When I first started on this journey, I could not qualify for a conventional bank loan. If you do not qualify for a loan from a traditional bank, follow my strategy:

1. Look up Credit Unions in your area. Credit Unions are usually more forgiving of their members than traditional banks are of their customers. Search Yelp and KreditKarma.com and look for reviews that include "They instantly gave me a huge line of credit." If a credit union give loans and credit easily, that usually indicates they are willing to lend for mortgages easily as well.

2. If you qualify for their terms, you can open an account with as little as $5 until you're ready to invest. If you are opening the account explicitly to apply for a loan, deposit additional funds to show you are going to be a good

business partner. I suggest $2,000 – $4000+, which should be a part of your investment stash. It only matters that you are a member of a Credit Union; it doesn't matter how significant your buy-in is.

3. Military-oriented banking institutions tend to be more liberal with lending than other institutions.

4. Ask investors with experience investing in this price range for national lender recommendations.

If Credit Unions don't work for you, or if there isn't one in your area that you can use, there are still other options. If you have a 401k, you can take out a 10k-15k loan (that's all you need per property if you are getting a mortgage). You can use your tax refund as a down payment. You can also use whatever personal savings you have.

The beauty of this price range is that you only put a relatively small amount of money "at risk" (*"at risk"* being a loose term, since we minimize all risks with knowledge and foresight) for gaining a large annual return and monthly cash flow.

Don't get me wrong – I'm not telling you to take on high-interest credit card debt, title pawn your car, or use unsecured debt to finance real property. Instead, I'm saying that you can float short term-debt using smart strategies. Let's say you have $1,000 in savings, and you are getting a $2,500 tax refund. That's $3,500. Then, take a $2,500 loan from your 401k, and that gives you the $6,000 you need for the 20% down payment for a $30,000 house. But wait! You need to do $2,000 in repairs and renovations! Most big home improvement stores like Home Depot and Lowe's will give you a 'same as cash' credit option for three to six months.

So, go ahead and charge those items for repairs and renovations. By the time you have to pay it back or before interest starts accruing, you will be getting cash flow from rent.

If you own your car outright, you may be able to leverage the equity in your car to get a loan. I wouldn't suggest going through a high-interest title pawn company. Those loans are so expensive that you run a very real risk of losing your car when and if you can't make the payments. You may be able to get a good loan with a reasonable interest rate from a Credit Union. For my second investment property, I got a $10,500 loan on my car at only a 4% interest rate from a Credit Union. Between that and the retail credit cards from Home Depot and Lowe's, I was able to purchase and renovate my second property. I did that three times! Each time I paid off the loan and was able to repeat the process when I had a new house to buy.

Personal loans are an excellent option for those with not-so-good credit, but higher cash flow and income. A Credit Union may give you a personal, unsecured loan. It doesn't hurt to ask – the worst thing they can say is no. And sometimes they say yes – it has worked for me. It was easier once I established myself as someone who paid their loans. The only caveat with a personal loan is that the payment is much higher than other credit card or mortgage payments, so you can only have one or two out at a time and cannot scale to as many properties as you can with a mortgage. I had perfect credit, was making six figures as an IT consultant, and had little debt, but I could not qualify for a personal loan because the payment was so high, although I could pay the amount five times over. So, one personal loan at a time and your rate of acquisition would be every two years. But if you have a foreclosure like me, personal loans are a great option while you wait seven years for your foreclosure to age enough to qualify for a mortgage. I paid off two homes this way.

And, for short-term financing, you can use retail credit cards. For instance, Lowes and Home Depot also contract to do home renovation tasks. Roofs, gutters, doors, windows, flooring, cabinets, etc. All of these can be purchased with their credit cards, which give 18 to 24 months financing to pay it off (with the rents, of course). I've used over $17,000 in short-term financing like this through big-box retailers and through mom and pop vendors.

Did you know that when searching Angie's list, you can filter based on which contractor company offers financing? I got a Wells Fargo home improvement card that offered 36 months financing through a contractor. Some contractors go above and beyond to be listed as an approved merchant of these credit lines and offer financing. Yes, I have used this extensively, and once the card was paid off, I was able to see which other merchants in that area also utilized that financing arm. And, I noticed they were higher quality merchants as well. You put these items together, you really have the money to fund any renovation you need to, so use it sparingly and as a way to buy time.

You can use any combination of those options. I used all four for my investment property in Baltimore, MD.

At the time, I utilized all of these options, and I still had the foreclosure on my credit report. I had an OKAY credit score (620-660). But I was creative and able to make it work. You can, too.

And best of all? All these personal loans and lines of credit are easy to consolidate and refinance as needed. So, once the free financing offer expires, it's easy to go to any bank (even the local ones) and ask for a credit card consolidation loan (they will include the retail cards and personal loans). When they took what I paid, extended over five years, it lowered the payment $151 the first time I tried this. I paid the minimums for another year, and when I consolidated it the second time (again, they took what was left and extended it over five years for a refinanced consolidated loan), the payment went down another $241. So, there ARE options, and there is a strategy behind this – that even a foreclosure didn't stop!

FINANCING YOUR RENTAL PROPERTY

Here's some basic information about the pros and cons of some different financing options. It doesn't matter who you are – if you are someone who has a half a million dollars sitting in an investment account or someone who makes $15.00 an hour, there are financing options that fit your needs if you know where to look.

CASH PURCHASES

Obviously, the easiest way to buy a house is to hand over the cash. Not everyone can do that, but more people than you'd think can with this Sub-30k method. I helped one woman who worked two jobs in a hospital cafeteria. She didn't make much money, but she had a roommate to help keep her expenses low. She was able to save 50% of her take-home pay and buy her first house with cash!

The main advantage to a cash purchase is that after taxes, insurance, and repairs, all your income is pure cash flow. You can also get your house for a better price. Most sellers would rather have your cash in hand in a couple of weeks rather than wait more than a month for the financing and evaluations to be done by the bank, especially since that may fall through, delaying the sale even further.

The main disadvantage is that it takes too long to save up that amount for many people. So, if you have your nest egg and can purchase a few houses using this method, go for it. However, if it will take you another five years to save this amount, I would recommend using mortgages or a combination of personal loans to build your portfolio.

CONVENTIONAL MORTGAGES

Mortgaging your investment properties is the fastest way to build your portfolio on the front end, and, therefore, the fastest way to multiplying cash flow.

This method works best for people who have clear credit and a solid work history, or two plus years of self-employment. It isn't easy or great if you take a lot of deductions from your taxes.

You generally need a 20% down payment, but in this market, you're only talking about $6,000 to $10,000. It is usually easier to come up with that amount than the entire purchase amount.

Some mortgage companies don't want to get involved in the lower end markets. I worked with one bank that wouldn't lend to my client for less than $100,000. In this case, you can re-target your goal and buy a multi-family house with several units. I adjusted my client's expectations, and instead of getting three houses in the $30,000 range, I got one house with three units in the $100,000 range. In the end, it worked out the same, and I was able to get better financing from a more reputable lender.

PERSONAL LOAN

Personal loans can be good, but should not be the end all be all, if for no other reason than the interest rates and terms are not usually the lowest. These loans can work for you, however, if you can't get a traditional mortgage. You must have high cash flow projections to make it work or be prepared to have negative cash flow for some time until you pay off some of that loan. This is because personal loans have higher installment payments than a traditional mortgage, and require more time to pay down the principle. Your credit only needs to be in the good/fair category.

Using personal loans will delay your accumulation of properties due to their high payments. However, you can refinance every year to reduce the payments and interest rate. When you are getting these loans, always try to get the longest-term length they offer – that will keep your payments as low as possible.

I would only use this strategy until you can qualify for a traditional mortgage. It is a holding pattern to use while you accumulate your first properties, so the inability to qualify for a traditional mortgage doesn't stop you indefinitely.

I used personal loans when I first started investing. I couldn't get a traditional mortgage because of my foreclosure. But I did have a job, and I was single, so I was able to keep my personal expenses very low. When that was successful, I tried to get a second personal loan for a second property, and I was denied. I was told that if I already had one, I couldn't have two. I only got away with having two personal loans at once one time, and that was when I applied at four places on the same day. Two approved me, and the inquiries on my credit report did not count against me. I had two loans. There's that hustle working for me again!

If you use a personal loan, refinance every one to two years. After you've made twelve months of on-time payments, lenders will see that you are someone who pays their bills. Banks are usually comfortable with unsecured debt like personal loans (they consider the same as credit card debt). If they see that kind of track record of on-time payment, they may refinance and consolidate your credit debt (usually along with any other credit card debt you have) and offer a new loan term and interest rate – both of which lower the monthly payment with that refinance.

This is a good way to start. It is a way to get your feet wet in real estate investing and get comfortable with it. By the time you have established enough credit and income to use more traditional financing methods, you've already started your empire.

HARD MONEY LENDERS

I am not a big fan of hard money lenders for this type of investment. They are for people with bad credit, no credit, and/or no money. Few will lend long term – the longest I've ever seen is 60 months, which is five years. They charge very high interest rates (12–15% – a personal loan is usually 7%-14%). This type of loan is something you would use if you are flipping or wholesaling houses and only need the loan for a very short term.

Be careful with hard money lenders. They can get you in a lot of trouble. It isn't cheap, and they're going to want a 20-30% down payment, so you have to bring money to the table, too. If you miss a payment, it can trigger a provision that makes the entire loan due at once.

401k AND RETIREMENT ACCOUNTS

A lot of people get nervous dipping into their 401ks to invest, but if can work for you if you know how to do it right.

You would, of course, act very differently if you had $400,000 socked away in your 401k vs. $40,000.

Let's say you have $400,000. You could take out only 25% and pay cash for three houses with that money. In no time at all, you'd make more money on those three houses each month than you would on your entire portfolio in a year.

Be aware that sometimes there are tax or other penalties for taking money out of your 401k, especially if you are under 59½ years old. Do the math. Some of those penalties will be offset by the expenses and early term losses of your real estate business. They may cancel each other out. A lot of that depends on structuring your parent company and your real estate investing arm of your business well. More on sophisticated business structuring in Chapter 10 "Accounting and Bookkeeping."

HOME EQUITY LINE OF CREDIT

A home equity line of credit, sometimes called a HELOC, is when you use the equity in a home you already own to finance the new home. This can work well because if you can pull out enough equity you might not have to come up with a down payment and get another mortgage.

How much equity you can pull out of your house depends on your lending institution. Some will only allow you to borrow up to 80% of the equity, some will go as high as 95%. Credit unions tend to let you take more.

You can do it in two ways – you can refinance the whole mortgage plus some and take cash out for reserves. I admit I tend to do this. If I don't use the cash, I just pay it back. Some people prefer a line of credit to use at will. This can work great, but I remember back in 2008 when the market crashed, and the banks were telling people that hadn't used their lines of credit that they could no longer take money out of them. If we have another financial crisis, that might be a problem. Of course, the problem with taking all the money out in the front end is that you have to pay interest on the whole amount from the get-go. There are pros and cons for each strategy.

To sum up financing and purchasing rental properties in general, the best real estate advice I can give you is, "To get started, just start!" Don't let other people's vision of real estate investing shape yours. No matter who you are, you can make this happen if you want it to happen. Take your vision and use it to build your dreams. Set your own goals, and figure out what you need to do to get there. Talk to your mentor to brainstorm ways to get around potential obstacles, and what are the best options for YOUR financials - not the internet's or someone else's. Do what makes you feel comfortable because you are the only one who knows exactly what you need.

ANALYZING CASH FLOW

Conventional wisdom will tell you that the value of the property itself is the most important thing to consider when investing in property. That's great advice if you have 20 years to wait to pay it off and pray for appreciation. I'm here to tell you that's not true: it's the cash flow. Cash flow is entirely dependent upon the rent that will be coming in compared to the monthly cost of owning the property.

The advice about A class neighborhoods, or that the house value is more important than the cash flow for rentals is good advice for rich people – when you can wait 30 years to pay the house off to get great cash flow. If you're reading this book – you probably don't have a $500,000 bank account, nor do you want to wait 30 years to get $1500 a month in cash flow. So, we need to look at those figures today, immediately upon placing the house into service.

Remember, we want an income-producing asset, not a drain on our expenses. We're in it for the long haul, true, but we shouldn't have to sacrifice our present for some future goal. This property should be purchased and renovated at such a low price that you're almost guaranteed cash flow right away. That's one of the things I teach first in my online courses and mentoring – how to do the math. You need to know how to add up the common expenses like insurance, taxes, routine maintenance and repairs, and mortgage, and balance it against the rent that will be coming in.

The expenses are easy to calculate, but in this price range, nuance is everything. So, I will go over the numbers and will follow up with what you should expect to receive as far as monthly gross (and net) income.

Monthly Rent		0	
EXPENSES	**Annual**	**Monthly**	
Property Taxes			(Can usually find this online)
Insurance			(typically $30-$60)
Property Management			(typically 8-10%)
Mortgage			(Dependent On Financing)
Renovation Credit Lines			(Dependent On Financing)
HOA			(Dependent On HOA community)
Vacancy (10% of rents)			
Repairs(5% of rents)			(Can base it off a 10% rate)
TOTAL			
Cashflow (Monthly Rent- Monthly Expenses):			

CashFlow	
Minimum Cashflow	**$150**
Good Cashflow	$250
Fantastic Cashflow	$350 and up
Pre-filled Calculations (Do Not Enter Value Directly)	

MONTHLY CASH FLOW

Monthly Rent _____

- Property Taxes (can usually find this online) _____
- Insurance (typically $30-$60) _____
- Property Management (typically 8-10%) _____
- Mortgage (Dependent on financing options) _____
- HOA fees (dependent on HOA community) _____
- Renovation Credit Lines (dependent on financing) _____

Gross Cash flow = _____

- Vacancy Rate (10%) _____
- Repairs (5%) _____

Net Cash flow = _____

NET VERSUS GROSS CASH FLOW

Gross cash flow is how much cash you have in your bank account after mandatory expenses. You have to pay the mortgage,

Homeowners Association (HOA) fees, insurance, etc. Most investors consider this as the most important number, as you can let this accumulate in your bank account, to help assist with your next investment.

Net cash flow involves putting away 15% for future repairs and vacancy expenses. The net cash flow can look significantly different.

I use the gross cash flow first because at this stage I am not living off the cash flow and I can just let it all sit in the pot, and use it towards future purchases and/or repairs. However, if you choose to move off of the net income to be even more conservative, there is nothing wrong with that either. The goal is to pay off these homes and retain 80%-90% of the monthly rents, not just a portion. Because of that, most investors just put it all in the pot.

It's important to make sure that you earn enough in rents annually to justify the expense. If you only earn $500 total in rents each month – even if you own the property free and clear, that's $6000 a year – you'll have to make sure there are no major repairs on the horizon. One $3,000 HVAC replacement or (periodic) or one $3500 roof replacement (natural disasters) can wipe out an entire year of income. So, that low rent depends on how much work that home needs.

My minimum cash flow (gross) that I would accept for a unit is $350. I will accept $300 if someone is investing in the south – the demographics of that region has lower rents in general outside of major cities. That has enough padding to save for future investments, or any unexpected repairs on the building until the home is paid in full.

$250 is a decent cash flow. There are the "A Class Neighborhood" Investors who are used to that amount of cash flow (or less). $150 is the absolute minimum that is acceptable. And that's only because you are not willing to travel out of state (in a non-local to your area).

This is the system that I teach, and we go from there. Anything less is garbage in my mind, even if it will appreciate in 30 years – that's not on my timeline, financial freedom in two to four years is.

CASH FLOW AS COMPARED TO PRICE POINT

The amount of cash flow NEEDS to be towards the higher end, regardless of how much the rental property cost, but especially if you're shelling out a ton of money for the property.

While speaking at the REI Expo in DC, I remember a conversation with an investor who was struggling to find a property. Taking the cookie-cutter advice you find on major forums, he searched for a rental property close to where he lived. Living in Northern Virginia (that has two of the most expensive counties in the country), the only property that was affordable was a $240,000 condo that would cash flow (gross) $200 a month.

Let me explain why this is a bad idea. First, if you're going to gross $200 a month, let's make sure you paid less than 50k for the home, not $240,000 for that type of monthly return.

Yes. It matters.

Second, the down payment expense for a condo at that price is 20% – that's $48,000. You can purchase a rental outright for that amount of money, and earn anywhere from $1000-$1500 a month – not $200. At those rents, one six- to eight-week vacancy can wipe out a year's worth of earnings.

That's the difference. Traditional advice is tinged with classism and privilege. Classism in the fact that entire neighborhoods of working-class people are ignored and stereotyped. Privilege because the people giving advice are telling people that it's a good idea to spend $48,000 to get a rental, and wait 30 years to get the property free and clear. Not everyone has the luxury of putting that sort of money down to wait 30 years and make $200 a month. You must be very comfortable to give advice to someone who has spent ten years saving up 20k – to tell them that's not enough or that they need 30k more to live the life of their dreams. That's a bit of privilege, and that's why I had to speak up on a different path to financial freedom that's a lot more affordable.

If your investment advice is for someone that has 150k in the bank and access to more through their mom and dad, then let them know your message is for people with deep pockets. And don't tell anyone they are wrong for investing in a lower-priced property in a working-class neighborhood – just because you're uncomfortable doesn't mean that others will be investing in that subclass.

You do NOT have to wait for 30 years; you don't need $50,000 to start. You can have your dream life and passive income in one to four years. That's it. That's your dream.

CHAPTER 6

Finding Tenants in Working Class Neighborhoods

Finding good tenants is key to having a profitable real estate investment business. After all, they are the ones that pay the rent that make up the cash flow.

There are some markets you will want to avoid entirely unless you're applying appreciation strategy and not cash flow. New York City, for example, has laws that are so tenant-friendly that it takes too long (and is incredibly expensive) to get rid of a tenant that doesn't pay rent or is otherwise destructive. I have stories of people who went in alone, and their retirement plan went up in flames because they weren't prepared for a yearlong eviction battle. That does not happen in Georgia – 30 days, you don't pay, you're out. In tenant-friendly areas in the northeast (Baltimore, New York, New Jersey), you will find yourself dealing with 'professional' tenants who have learned how to work the system and live for free as long as they can. You want to avoid that. Your job is to give people a quality place to live at a reasonable rent – not for free.

In a working-class neighborhood, you should understand the kind of tenant you are going to encounter. You can expect your rent to be paid every month; however, also expect that it will be late once or twice a year.

You can go to sites like BiggerPockets to get information about Real Estate investing and get some good advice. But the advice isn't really geared towards people like you and me, and this demographic. It isn't geared towards lower-priced homes in working-class neighborhoods, and so sometimes it is not quite right when you try to apply it to these markets. It's not bad advice; it just doesn't always apply in these situations. When you are starting out, it is easy to get confused by the conflicting advice you will get. I see investors time and again going on these major forums and asking elite investors who wouldn't be caught dead in a lower income neighborhood for advice on a lower income neighborhood – do you see the extreme disconnect? How is someone who doesn't even like that asset class supposed to advise you on navigating it?

It would be great if these investors said, "I haven't had success in these areas, nor do I invest in them, so you should ask someone who does have experience." I haven't ONCE seen that thoughtful response. I HAVE seen "Don't purchase a Sub30k PIG," or "Those neighborhoods are nothing but trouble," or "The people in those neighborhoods – you'll spend more time evicting than collecting rent." Or even "You should go to an A class neighborhood that's close to home and start there." All of this can be terrible advice. Neighborhoods are different. One neighborhood may have evictions every week, and another one is full of families that have been there for 18+ years. They both cost the same, but a discerning investor can pick the difference between the two. The advice you see in general doesn't have that level of discernment. Which is why I wrote this book. So many people have been left out of the conversation because of this arrogance – so I'm inviting all y'all in! No one is keeping me from the table ever again!

Remember: they aren't wrong in general, they just have no success or experience in these neighborhoods, but neither do they preface their advice with that information.

So, what do you need to look for in a hardworking tenant?

APPLICATION

It's important to have a good application process that will collect all the information you need. My property managers do this groundwork for me and then present it to me for the final decision. I want to know all about their income, their job history, their living history, their credit, their criminal history, and whether they've had civil lawsuits filed against them. If I don't get this information on the front end, and then I get a tenant that isn't a good one, it's on me. It is my job to ask the right questions and do a preliminary investigation. I can't expect a potential tenant to just volunteer this information.

INCOME AND CREDIT REPORT

The absolute, unchangeable rule is that people need to earn three times the amount of the rent. This is where nuance comes in. I will go down to 2.5 times the rent in income if they have a partner and good credit. If not, you're doing a disservice to them, putting them in a place where it isn't financially feasible (especially in the current environment of stagnant wages and rapid inflation). If the rent is $500 a month, they need to earn $1,500 a month. If the rent is $1,000 a month, they need to earn $3,000 a month. Period. No exceptions. It can be two people on the lease that make that happen (husband and wife team). But this isn't unreasonable at all to do, and it's mutually beneficial for both. Be firm on this, or you will regret it.

And news flash – if you can't find anyone that will qualify at that rent after two months...guess what...lower the rent to get another flock of possibilities.

This is not just to benefit you as the landlord, but to help the tenant. I've bent this rule in the past and been sorry about it. If they don't earn three times the rent, they can't afford the rent, and they end up getting stuck and making uncomfortable compromises with food and transportation. And when they have children, it's not a pretty sight for either party in this transaction. They get over-leveraged and stressed and can't handle the situation. No one wins when someone takes on more than they can afford. It isn't right on any level to put someone in a situation in which they are being set up to fail. No one wins, and everyone loses.

I'm not as strict with credit reports. In my neighborhoods, not everyone has perfect credit. If you have one charge off (charge off is a credit report term meaning they did not pay the bill and it was charged off and still outstanding), you might not even know what it is for. One blemish does not make the tenant a terrible prospect. If an applicant has several blemishes or charge-offs, though, DO NOT LET THEM IN. It means they are okay with not meeting their obligations. This is a pattern for them, and you do not want to be a part of that pattern. One I can understand. Two? Maybe under certain circumstances with a good explanation. Three or more? Not at all. Will they try to rent your house? Yes, they just want to get in to try to ride it as long as possible. If you have one blemish and great references, you're ok by me. I will let you in. The credit report is not the be all and end all for me. But I will NOT let you take advantage of me just because you can make up a good sob story. We all have troubles. I am under no obligation to take on your troubles to my own financial detriment.

JOB STABILITY

It isn't enough that someone has a job that pays enough to cover the rent, they must have a history of having a job that covers the rent. Anyone can *get* a job – it's keeping a job that is the trick. If you have had your job for at least a few months, I'm probably open to you as a tenant. If you've just had it for a few weeks, I'm going to want to dig further. If you had a job for years, and then recently switched to a better paying job, that's ok. If you were unemployed for years, that's *not* ok. I need to know that you are stable and that your ability to earn an income is stable. Otherwise, I'll have to deal with the fallout, and I'm not interested in that. There is little leeway on job history, though it is one of those things that you can use your gut feeling on.

It's ok to ask questions, but be sure you are not violating any discrimination laws when you ask the questions. Sometimes, for example, a woman has been unemployed for many years because she was married and relied on her husband for support, and now she is recently divorced or widowed. Or maybe she stayed home with her children because daycare costs more than she could earn, and now they are old enough to go to a free public school. Depending upon the situation, it may be something reasonable that you can work with. This is one of those kinds of situations where your gut instinct can control. The more you do this, the more finely tuned your gut will be, and you'll know when you can make exceptions. Until then, bounce it off your mentor and see what she thinks.

REFERENCES

We check references, and they are important. Good references can overcome a lot of other negatives. Always check people's references, and ask pointed questions. If you have a blemish or two on your credit, but you have good references, that's reasonable, and you should be able to work with that – it's seen in this demographic where wages are tight, and inflation is high.

When I talk to references, I always ask how many times in a 12-month period the person has been late paying their bills. If it is a time or two, that's ok. Anyone can be late a time or two. But three or more? That's a red flag I will not ignore. There's late, and there's *late*. When they are late, are they a day or two late, or are they a month or two late? Do you have to chase them down for the payment, or do they come with it on their own with an apology and maybe a plate of homemade cookies? I have a retired couple in one of my properties who are almost never late, and when they are, they make sure to let my property management company know why and when they will make it up (usually if there is a misstep in social security payments which happens occasionally).

I don't know about you, but I don't want to have to chase money. My job is to provide the place to live; their job is to pay for it. It should be that simple.

But let's be clear – references only go so far. Keep in mind that if they are a horrible tenant, their current landlord may say they are "just fine," so that they will leave their place. Everyone talks about telling the truth and integrity until they have a tenant who always has an excuse and never pays. It's cheaper and easier to just say, "They were an alright tenant" than to tell the truth. So, references only go so far, if you can get in contact with them.

You don't have to be scared, but just understand – I have found wonderful tenants without contacting their references. The details of who they are make up more of the story. A father who is a coach at the local high school and has a daughter he watches full time. A retired couple on social security. A family of four with the mom and dad present. And yes, a single mother who was an insurance adjuster. Their story and credit report provided more insight into what kind of tenants were moving in more than any reference.

You always need to put things in perspective when working with a different demographic.

EVICTIONS AND COURT RECORDS

I will not accept a tenant with a recent history of evictions and lawsuits based on credit. There are many reasons for this. The most obvious is because if they've done it before, they will do it again. If they've forced one landlord to go to court to get them out, they will force another. If they've forced one person to sue them to get their money, they will force another. If you don't believe me, then you try it.

But there's another, more practical reason, and that's this: I don't want to be second in line behind someone to get my money. I once rejected a potential tenant because she had an active judgment against her. I didn't want to take her on because what if I had to sue her? I couldn't garnish her wages because someone was already doing it, and I don't want to have to wait. It is too much work, and I want my money now so I can keep this property maintained.

The public records aren't always clear, and they aren't always 100% accurate, but there are enough tenants out there who don't have these issues to choose from that you don't have to bother with the ones who do.

However, there are circumstances in which I would consider someone with this record. Say you were a flight attendant who is living in motel rooms because you had an eviction (true story, real people). You have a well-paying job you didn't have before and can provide an explanation. In this case, if the reason they were evicted sounds reasonable, I may offer them rent if they pay the maximum in security deposit (that's two to three months' rents, it differs per city), and first and last month's rent. If you do have to evict for non-payment again, you at least have the security deposit and last month's rent to recover your cost. I would do that in a heartbeat, but you can understand – they have a higher threshold to partner with you in business, and prove they can now meet their financial obligations.

NOT HARD AT ALL TO GET GREAT, UPSTANDING TENANTS

Federal Housing Laws *Familiarize yourself with these laws*

There are many Federal Housing Laws involving discrimination, and it is important that you don't violate them, especially in your application process. Federal agencies have people who will act as 'mystery shoppers' to see if you are doing the right thing. Don't try to be nice, don't try to give tips. Just stick to the facts and be professional. Read the discrimination laws and make sure you are compliant[7].

One time, I had someone call me and ask if I had "things for a wheelchair." I didn't give any unnecessary information; I only gave them the phone number for the property manager so they could get an application. I didn't say, "Well, um, the bathroom is small, and I don't know if a wheelchair will fit in there." I just told them where they could go to fill out an application. My property manager knows the laws better than I do – that's why I hired a property manager! Because I knew I had the right team, I referred this potential tenant to the right team member who could handle this for me. The housing authority sends undercover agents around asking this question just to fine people who are violating the laws and to send a message to other landlords. With a little bit of foresight, it is very easy to avoid trouble. Side note – with the aging population, investing in a ramp and wheelchair accessibility is lucrative, so do not underestimate this avenue for cornering a steady stream of tenants.

SUMMARY

The stricter you are in choosing who your tenants will be based on practical advice for this financial demographic, the fewer problems you will have down the road. I'm strict on income, job history, and court records, but will give an option for higher deposits and upfront fees to defray the cost of credit issues if the reasons for the issues are reasonable. I like having "upstanding citizens" in my properties.

---

[7] The Fair Housing Act can be found here: https://www.justice.gov/crt/fair-housing-act-2 and you can find more information at the federal government's website for the Department for Housing and Urban Development.

Now you know how to find your perfect home, and how to find the perfect tenant to put in it! Understand the reality of this socio-economic demographic, and everyone will be in a win/win situation.

FINANCIAL FREEDOM FOR ONE MOM, A SAFE HOME FOR ANOTHER

Janelle wasn't afraid to work. An immigrant to this country, she had two jobs from the time she was 17 years old. That was just life; it was the way it was for her own mother who had to make do without assistance from anyone, and the way it was going to be, or so she thought. Then she got married, and she and her husband wanted to start a family. She thought about her life in the future. She wanted to be with her daughter in the evenings, not working second shift in a restaurant. She wanted to be able to give her daughter what she didn't have – a mother who was present, who could sign her up for ballet lessons and soccer.

Janelle knew there had to be another way. She found my videos on YouTube. She told me later that at first she thought it must be a scam. But she watched more and watched real people give their testimonials, and she finally reached out to me.

I helped Janelle find a house within a half hour's drive from her own house for $34,000. She fixed it up herself for very little money, and almost immediately found a woman with two small daughters to rent it. This woman reminded Janelle of her mother, hard-working and scrappy and just looking for a break. She told me later that she wasn't sure what she liked more – getting the rent checks every month or knowing that her tenant's daughters were sleeping safely in the bedroom that she painted for them.

Now, Janelle owns three houses and has two daughters of her own. She only works part-time, and the rest of her income comes from her rental properties. Heaven is rental property ownership with great tenants.

There is definitely a spiritual and compassionate aspect you can incorporate into your investment strategy, and I absolutely want you to be mindful of that when investing. You are providing someone a stable home in exchange for rent, and you should absolutely tell people you not only have created the life of your dreams, but you did it in a way that makes you feel blessed to offer this home to people who can use some kindness and fair play coming their way.

CHAPTER 7

Property Managers Are Key

WHY USE A PROPERTY MANAGER?

When investing in working-class neighborhoods that you don't live in, property managers are the key to success.

Since I live in the Washington D.C. area, which doesn't have a whole lot of affordable real estate investment opportunities, I look to neighboring cities and states with more affordable options. These can be from 30 to 90 to even 400 miles away. Staying local and investing in an "A class" neighborhood may mean a $100,000 down payment to make $300 in cash flow a month. I'm not paying that amount of money for that payday, so Out of State (or out of city) investing it is!

I couldn't do this without having a licensed, qualified, and skilled property manager on my team. A property manager is a person (or business) that takes care of finding tenants for your rental property, deals with the day-to-day maintenance of the property, responds to tenant concerns, and, when necessary, files evictions. In other words, they handle the business for you while you sit back and collect the cash flow.

I can be a rental property owner without being a landlord. It's really up to you. People are different.

I am someone who truly wants the passive income lifestyle. I want the income, but I don't want to replace my job for another. I want it all. That's why before we invest in a market with my clients who are out of state, we make sure we're clear on their goals and ensure there are several options for property management teams before we look at homes. More on that topic in Chapter 9 – *"Investing Out of State."*

Some people want to be "hands on" and do the work. My husband is one of them. He wants to take the call and call the repairman himself. If that's you, then it's not as important to make sure there are ample property management companies to choose from. Instead, he can rely on an airtight contract and have a clause for anything that happens spelled out clearly to assist your efforts. This book is for anyone who wants the passive income, without the job of investing or being a "landlord" in the traditional sense. I call myself an investor and rental property owner.

Property management is a mature industry that used to be done exclusively by a friend of the family or real estate agent for a side income. However, as real estate investment has grown, this has become an industry of its own. This new industry has become a key player in facilitating the passive real estate income we are looking for.

In theory, property managers should make your real estate investing smooth. They should free you up and allow your portfolio to show geographic diversity since you don't have to be on site to manage the property or field maintenance calls.

I say "in theory," because this only works if you have a skilled property manager. A bad one, an inefficient one, or one who simply won't do his or her job can cause you as much stress as if you had to do all the work yourself.

I can get a property in most cities and will pass on investing in a location if there isn't a presence. If you don't want to worry about a property a hundred miles away, or even half a country away, property management is your answer. I rely heavily on property management so that I don't have to worry about any of the day-to-day management including court filings in the event of eviction, rent collection, and minor repairs. I can be on vacation drinking wine in the South of France or enjoying the sun on the beach in Jamaica while the rent checks keep coming in with the help of a great property manager. The first of the month comes whether or not I'm on site.

I was on a grand vacation in New Zealand, reuniting with my now husband after he spent a year in Afghanistan. I received an email from my property management company that the air conditioning broke in a rental in Richmond, VA. My management handled it and told me it would cost about $250 for the repair. It was fixed promptly; my tenants were happy. I was happy it didn't cost too much, and my vacation wasn't ruined. That's the life you get with the right property management team, and why it's important to take it into account before acquiring your first property.

you don't want to pay for a vacant property.

I learned how to do this like I learned most things – the hard way. I learned that bad or unscrupulous property managers charge a monthly fee even when the property is vacant – sometimes even the *same* monthly fee. This is a bad business model for you because what incentive do they have to fill the property? They get paid the same, and they don't have to do any work when the property is vacant. Some of them will feed you some lines – *we're showing the place; we're advertising the place; we should get paid for that.* But it isn't true. There are better management companies that don't get paid when it is vacant, and why should they? Often, they are simply listing the property as vacant, and other agents are doing the actual showing. My advice is this: Choose another management team if they charge for vacant properties unless they have an absolutely spotless reputation.

I had property in Baltimore, and I was about to call it quits I was so frustrated. I was so close to cashing in my investments due to a lack of competence in the team I had there. Many of the property managers were charging me when the house was vacant. Even during the prime summer months, the houses were sitting empty. I *knew* they weren't doing their jobs, and I was at my wit's end.

That's when I found out about NARPM, pronounced NAR-pam. NARPM stands for the National Association of Rental Property Managers and can be found at www.narpm.org. Keep this amazing resource handy, and use it whenever you invest in properties in a new city. You can go to the website and plug in a zip code or the name of a city and see how many property managers are registered. If they have none or only one or two, you might want to stay away. If they have a lot, you're good. For example, a city like Savannah, Georgia, which has a lot of low-cost, high-rent properties, has 12 hits on NARPM. That means you'll probably go a long way there. My other two go-to sources to find high-quality property management is Angieslist.com and BBB.org (Better Business Bureau).

When I found out about NARPM, I sent a blanket email to all the people listed on the site for Baltimore and found a solid property management group.

A lot of you, like me, simply can't find low cost, high rent properties in the cities in which you live. Low cost, high rent properties do exist in nearby Baltimore, MD and Richmond, VA, however. I can make it work because I have a solid, licensed property management group in place in each location that can deal with the properties for me. It makes everything, even the rehab of new properties, easy.

I'm more established in Richmond, and everything is perfectly smooth there and also in my Columbus property. Baltimore is a special case, but I can tell you more about it in my Facebook group *Sub30k Mastermind Group*

Facebook.com/groups/Sub30kMastermindGroup.

When you start with a new property management team, make sure you read the entire contract and ask questions. Have a template of questions that you ask every single time to make sure that you are consistent. (See below where I talk about what to ask a property manager and why you should ask those questions.) I usually get a list of ten possible management companies and email the list to all of them in one session. It's that easy. Because you know what to ask, and WHY you are asking that.

Once you are working with a good property management company, it should be easy. The rent should come at regular intervals. They may call you with questions from time to time, or send you email updates. When something goes awry, they should take care of it without involving you if it isn't anything major. They will tell you about it after the fact. That's what you are paying them to do.

The more systems you have in place, the more you make money even when you are sleeping. Property management is one of those systems.

There's a book called *Why "A" Students Work for "C" Students and Why "B" Students Work for the Government* written by Robert Kiyosaki. One of the premises of that book is that "A" students work hard – but "C" students are masters at getting other people to do the hard work for them. "A" students have something to learn from "C" students about time management. Do a cost-benefit analysis and recognize that time is money. Let someone else do the work for you. Why are you dealing with late rent and a malfunctioning pilot light in a gas heater when a property management company could be dealing with it for you?

Real estate investment is more than just having the money to invest in real estate. It's a business, and it requires management. Management requires managers – property managers are professional managers who know their industries. Just like you hire a plumber to do plumbing, hire a property manager to do the property management! You can grow your real estate investment business faster and more efficiently that way.

Once you figure out the formula, each house becomes that much easier. Having a team in place just makes everything flow. When I bought my first house, I did everything myself. It was a lot of work – I was happy to do it to make my dreams come true, but it was exhausting. The last house I bought, all I did was buy the house – someone else did everything else, and all the work was done for me. Now all I do is read emails and respond accordingly. It is a lot smoother and a whole lot more passive. I can read an email from anywhere in the world. It's a lot better than my cubicle at IBM!

My goal is to own seven houses, all fully paid off. I am well on my way to that goal. And it feels wonderful.

WHAT TO ASK A PROPERTY MANAGER

Below, I have provided my standard list of questions that I ask property managers. When I ask these questions, instead of calling and asking, I will put them in an email. I send the same email out at the same time to all the property managers I am interviewing, Blind carbon copy (bcc) each of them so they don't know they aren't the only ones receiving the message. I tell them that I work during the day and can't receive phone calls, and so I prefer an emailed response. That makes it a lot easier to compare their answers. I can print them out and physically lay them side-by-side. It also makes sure that they answer the questions I'm asking instead of redirecting the conversation the way they want it to go or giving me their pre-planned sales pitch. This just saves time and is a more strategic way of accessing the possible talent.

Beneath the list of questions, I provide further explanations about the questions themselves, and why I have chosen those particular questions to include in my template. You can add to this list, or change it as you see fit to suit your needs, but just remember: I've compiled this list over years of trial and error. I've made a lot of mistakes along the way to get this finely tuned list that gets me the information I need. You can learn from my experience.

The Template:

1. What are your set up fees and the monthly fees after that?

Usually, the fees are 7-10% of the monthly rental fees. I'm willing to pay a little bit more for a property manager that is really good. It's about a "five" on a scale of one to ten of importance for me. I'm not money focused; I'm quality focused. If they charge a leasing fee, it might not influence me as much as if I know they are going to do what they say they are going to do. I will pay more for better results.

2. **My property is a ___ bedroom, ____ bathroom home located on _____ Street in _____, State. Have you rented in this area before? How long does it take you to fill vacancies in this area? Do you get mostly Section 8[8] renters or market renters for this area?**

It is important to me that the property managers I am dealing with are familiar with this particular market. Since I am dealing with working-class neighborhoods and lower income tenants, I want property managers that are experienced in dealing with these houses and these kinds of renters, and intimately understand the socio-economic culture. If you have a choice between someone who has experience in this area and someone who doesn't, take the person with experience every time. You want shorter vacancies, and someone who knows how to deal with Section 8 is going to be better at reducing the vacancy time and not mess it up along the way. I don't want the property managers to learn the process it on my back and on my time. In this market, there are a lot of people who already know how to do it. There are enough headaches that come with the territory – don't add another headache on top of everything. And definitely don't hire someone that is going to look down their nose at a working-class person

Make sure PMs are familiar with area

---

[8] Section 8 refers to Section 8 of the Housing Act of 1937, and it is a federal government program that provides housing assistance to poverty stricken and elderly Americans. It has guidelines that go along with it that must be followed, both by the renter and the landlord, in order for everyone to qualify. When done correctly, it can benefit both the tenant and the landlord.

trying to find a place to live. Not today. They aren't your ideal business partner.

3. What are your maintenance fees and limits?

This one is huge in my book, especially the limits. Sometimes, people will charge a low monthly fee and then make it up in what they charge you for repairs, either overcharging for repairs they do or taking a percentage of the repairs. I like the limit to be $250. This means that for any repair under $250, they don't have to get my approval. Some property managers want your approval for every little thing, and that doesn't work for me either – after all, isn't the whole point of having a property manager that you don't have to deal with everything that goes wrong? If you have to change a $5 fuse, don't bother me with it! On the other hand, I don't want them spending too much of my money without my consent. That's why I like the $250 limit. Don't be afraid to negotiate. If the contract they offer you says $500, ask if they will lower the threshold to $250. If they won't, I wouldn't do business with them. That number can vary depending on your comfort level. After doing this for many years, $250 is the number I've landed on that makes me comfortable. Your level of comfort may be different, and that's ok.

4. How many full- and part-time staff members manage your properties?

The 'right' answer to this question can vary, depending on the answer to the next question….

5. How many properties are do you manage?

One time I interviewed a property manager who managed one hundred properties, and he did it by himself. I wasn't impressed with that. That was too many, and I knew there was no way he

Make sure they can handle managing your property.

could focus on my properties. I interviewed another manager who had two hundred properties, but that was ok because he had a staff of ten people. I need to know that someone will be able to get back to me in a timely fashion and will be able to focus on my needs. One man teams are ok if they have a limited number of properties, say, under forty. But no more than that.

6. How many of the properties that you manage do you own?

I'm not a big fan of property managers owning the properties they manage. To me, it looks like a conflict of interest. It seems obvious that they will focus more on the properties in which they have a vested interest than on my properties. Also, it seems like they have more of an incentive to rent out their own properties before mine if both are vacant at the same time. If 25% or more of the properties that they manage are their own, it is a definite no. I prefer that they don't own *any* of the properties that they manage, but sometimes that just isn't realistic.

7. Is there an early termination fee if our mutual business needs aren't met?

No long term contract

I'm not a fan of contracts that I am stuck in for long periods of time. I already have a cell phone – a property management contract shouldn't be like a cell phone contract – I shouldn't have to pay hundreds of dollars if I want to get out in less than two years. And frankly, I don't know why they would want to be stuck with me, either. It doesn't benefit either the property management company or me to be stuck in an unsatisfactory business relationship. The more frustrated I am, the more likely I am to make a Better Business Bureau complaint, write a bad Yelp review, or file a civil lawsuit. That doesn't serve anyone's higher purpose. It is better for everyone if there is a 30-day 'escape' clause built into the contract. When you corner a tiger, that's when it is most ferocious – and when you corner me, that's when I'm most dangerous to you. There needs a way for both of us to get out if it isn't working for us.

Keep in mind that partnering with your real estate investment business is a soft art, and I am teaching you some skills to navigate. Don't assume everyone will take your business, and be cautious and protect yourself as much as possible in your contracts. These are rules to live by. If someone is great in all areas but wants a $500 threshold to fix problems themselves or contact you – weigh it against the other factors. It may well be the best decision if you compromise on some items and nurture a beneficial relationship you hope to last for many, many years. Don't be too strict, but you can be firm.

LIFE CHANGED AND A MOVE TO AN INVESTMENT RICH MARKET

CASE STUDY

David found my videos on YouTube and realized how easy it was to renovate houses using money borrowed from zero percent interest retail credit cards and then rent them out for instant cash flow. Using my formulas for finding houses and tenants, his monthly cost is about $350-$400 for each house. He brings in $750-$800 in rent. That's 100% profit! Using property managers, he can sit back and collect $400 *per month per house* with NO EFFORT! To speak to David and others, join our very supportive and welcoming group of investors in:

Facebook.com/groups/Sub30kMastermindGroup/

CHAPTER 8

Hiring Quality Contractors

You save money when you buy affordable houses in working-class neighborhoods, but you don't want to 'cheap out' when it comes to contractors. Choosing a contractor can be the best and most irritating aspect of real estate investing.

You bought the house, and that's great. But many times, you still need to do a lot more work before you can rent it out and start your cash flow. This can be a few minor repairs or a major renovation. Either way, the contractor search and gathering of estimates does get relatively smoother as you get better at sizing up your future 'temporary employees.' After doing this for a while, I have a new respect for hiring managers in corporate America. Finding good folks to do a job can be difficult when you're just starting out.

In this chapter, I'm going to talk about how you can weed out the good contractors from the bad contractors. When things go wrong – and they will go wrong, even with the best people – we'll talk about the best way to handle it to get the results you want. Throughout it all, remember: pictures are your best friend.

FINDING A FIVE-STAR CONTRACTOR

Like most people who have invested in rental properties, I have chosen the wrong contractors, but I quickly learned from my mistakes. So, you can take my advice and learn from my mistakes, or you can make them yourself: your choice. I feel like I say this a lot, but I've seen too many people ignore what I say and then regret it later. I don't want you to be in that position.

If you don't already have a contractor to work with that you trust, you have to search for one. Of course, the best way to find one is word of mouth. If you know someone who has had success working with someone in that local area, that's the best route to take. If that isn't possible (in the case that you are investing out of state and don't yet have an established network of real estate investors to bounce ideas off of), the two main 'search engines' I trust for this job are Service Magic and Angie's List. A lot of people prefer Service Magic because it's free, but I like Angie's List. It doesn't cost that much – just $35 tax deductible dollars a year. Not that Service Magic is bad, but in my experience, there is a level of professionalism that I consistently get with people who advertise on Angie's List that I don't get anywhere else (probably because it costs a little more to respond to any reviews left on Angie's list for the contractor). That's also good for you – if they are willing to pay to respond to reviews, that means they have learned how important an online reputation is. This is someone that is showing they care what the world thinks, and you like that because you know you can always post a review of bad performance, with pictures, to ensure a great end to your working relationship. It's win/win – you get someone who stands by their work and reputation, but also have some ammo (in addition to a great, well-defined contract) in case they don't deliver as promised. As a general rule, people who are willing to invest in themselves and their businesses take more pride in their work as a general rule.

I only talk with five-star rated contractors on Angie's List. Angie's List also has "Service Award" contractors. I'm not sure what their criteria is for awarding service awards, but if you can find someone who has won a service award, you can pretty much be guaranteed that person will offer great service.

I don't have the time to deal with people who have less than stellar reviews. Five-star ratings only. These are the people who care about pleasing their customers, and I am a customer who wants to be pleased. Sometimes – sometimes! – if someone has a lot of five-star reviews and one three-star review buried in there somewhere I will read the details of the three-star review to see if it is just some crabby person ranting that a phone call wasn't returned quickly enough for his or her taste. That I can live with. You can't please all of the people all of the time, but you can get a real feel for how this person operates from the reviews.

This reminds me of a story of when I was renovating my Richmond property. I have a wonderful property manager there, and asked her to check up on some work the general contractor performed (I didn't feel like making the two-hour round trip, and I had specifically contracted with her company to monitor the renovations as needed). She got there and looked at the flooring job – apparently, they missed the underlayment (that's the soft subflooring they put under for laminate flooring so it's padded), and that part of the floor clicked because it was empty space suddenly. Not the greatest work, right? She took a video right there on her phone and emailed it to me. I emailed it to the general contractor within five minutes of receiving it, and it was fixed the next day.

You see? An online contractor that cares about their reputation – they knew I could put that video up and show the work, contract, everything. So, they fixed it without an explanation and promptly. You had a system in place, so the property management checked up on a property you could not (or didn't want to) physically travel to. Check and mate. This all works out – especially because this was a five-star contractor who cared about those reviews.

Trust me – I've had some knuckleheads off craigslist who had multiple postings about how they were con-artists, but since it was just a post you couldn't tie them together. These online review sites really work.

A contractor that has a lot of solid five star reviews tends to be a little more expensive, but that's ok. You saved money on a $50,000 property versus $150,000 –pay the premium for quality work so you're not making repairs every five months. It won't usually be extravagantly higher, and in the long run, you will save money by not having to fix their mistakes or redo the work when it falls apart in a few years. I'm willing to pay for quality work. In the long run, it is worth it.

ESTIMATES

Once you've narrowed down your list of contractors for the job, get at least three estimates. The more, the better. You'll be surprised by the range you see. I could have a bid for doing a whole plumbing or roofing job, and it could range from $2,800 to $12,000. Seriously, I received those estimates for a plumbing job, and a range like that for the roof – for the same house. It's crazy! Sometimes I wonder why they even waste my time. You don't always get consistency with the smaller outfits. It took me a long time to realize that sometimes they don't actually want my business. Maybe they are swamped that week, or maybe their cousin is getting married out of state and they would rather not work. Sometimes they price themselves out of the game, figuring you probably won't bite, and if you do, they've hit the jackpot.

You will also learn the difference between a small general contracting outfit, and a major one. Some electricians and plumbers were single men who had a van and their tools. Some were like Roto-Rooter – a large local franchise with 12 vans and 30 people working. For the same job, there was a vast difference in price, quality, and speed. The smaller outfit may be cheaper but will take a week for a large job versus a day like the large contractor firm. All those factors can be defined, but you will have needs where speed (or just being available for emergency, night-time repairs) will be needed versus that not being a big factor. Respond accordingly and understand their overhead and expectations as well. I find when I do this, the business of us working together goes more smoothly because you're already accounting for that type of business – and aren't as shocked at the price tag.

Also with contractors – Don't get arrogant that people have to take your money on your terms. They don't! Some places there are only a limited amount of handyman companies, and they have plenty of work. If you guys don't click, they can be just as quick to turn down your business and simply not call back (or throw out a crazy high estimate) There are no guarantees! You have to build a relationship so that they want to do right by you. There is a way to do it without burning bridges if you are inclined (as I used to be) towards being extremely rigid.

At the end of the day, you have to trust your instincts. Talk to the contractors. Read the reviews. Ask to see pictures of jobs they've done. Nowadays, when everyone has a smartphone, there is no reason why they shouldn't be able to show you photos of the last few jobs they've done. Take it all in. They should be proud of the work they've done and happy to show you. They should be ready with a list of references. Look at the overall picture, and compare the estimates.

CONTRACTS

And about the estimates – contracts – make sure they are detailed. "Plumbing overhaul" may mean something different to you and to the plumber. Not too long ago, I got an estimate for a plumbing overhaul, and that's all it said. I sent an email back and said, "Your bid gave no details. I need to make sure it includes a front and back water hose, a shut-off valve, a shower fixture in the upstairs bathroom, a new sink in the laundry room, a drain in the kitchen," and I went on from there. I was very detailed. I've learned that if you don't write it out one of two things will happen: it either won't get done at all, or it will get done, and you will be charged extra because it "wasn't included in the original estimate." You write it up or have them write it up. Insist on it to make sure you got everything. Otherwise, you open yourself up for miscommunication. Articulate. Enumerate. This specific list is what I want included. Make sure they know that you will be mad if X isn't done or if you are charged extra for Y.

And, depending on the price point, directly written on the estimate (The contract), you should always have different parts they are responsible for and different draws. For example, for a 15k general contract job, I had three parts. I made the 1st payment when X was completed, the 2nd payment when the second phase was completed, and the third payment upon completion. For a 60k job, the estimate was in four parts of 15k each. The benefit of this is you only pay when the work has been completed to your satisfaction. If they don't do the first part right, then: 1) you don't pay for the second portion and 2.) you can hold them to the first part if you escalate it.

You can easily compare what was done to your detailed contract. Review what repairs were included in each phase. If replacing a toilet is listed and the contractor didn't do it – guess what – take a picture and escalate it as needed, but minimize your risk. This has been the single most important skill that I have learned and makes it so easy to manage a job. You get MULTIPLE payments, so we can part ways if needed. If you do nothing else, learn this skill – please. In the flow of conversation, they will get me a detailed estimate, and I will ask them to set it up in three draws, so that they get paid in three parts as they finish, and to schedule/order it in a way that makes sense. Everyone has done it, and it makes my life so much easier. Don't be worried, local or out of state, just get it in writing and be clear – you don't get paid for X until Y.

And let me tell you – they will ALWAYS ask for Y before they finish X. What that means is that you politely tell them, as I did, that per the contract, the payment for the next draw will not be made until the first part is complete. I had a general contractor that was a week behind schedule. When they asked for their money up front for the next section (as they inevitably do), I politely told them they don't get the next payment until this is done. Boy, let me tell you: They finished that section within two days and sent photos. That is power. That's how you position yourself for success. I can't go over everything in this book, that's what my 1-1 coaching and group coaching is for at affordable rates. (Schedule a call for a free strategy session here – http://lisa-phillips.thinkific.com/courses/1-on-1-mentoring) but this will put you on the path to success.

Another thing I've noticed is that high-rated contractors are better at working around your schedule. Recently I bought a house that needed both HVAC and plumbing work done. I had to coordinate those things – the HVAC workers and plumbers needed to be out of each other's way, and the plumbing needed to be out of the way of the ductwork. I was able to get them to talk to each other and work around each other's schedules. Then, when I changed my mind on what I wanted to do, they were flexible and worked with me. That's the advantage of working with quality folks who know you are not looking to nickel and dime you.

WHEN THINGS GO WRONG

Inevitably, something will go wrong. This is not only because of the law of averages but because contractors are humans and all humans occasionally make mistakes. Also, because of the nature of the industry, the people who work on the ground doing the hard work tend to rotate, and sometimes there are good workers there, and sometimes there aren't. It is hard to find good employees, especially when you are talking about backbreaking, difficult work like parts of construction can be.

So, what do you do? Since this is your house and your business and – hopefully – your passion project, you are likely to be mad that things are not going the way they should. That's natural and understandable. I'm not telling you that you shouldn't be mad. What I'm telling you is that the way you express your emotion will be the difference between getting a good result or just making things worse. Not everyone is excited about confrontation, especially with someone you've already paid to finish a job.

Sometimes you must escalate the issue. By 'escalate,' I don't mean resort to physical violence or anything drastic. I just mean take the method of resolution up to the next level. You hired a contractor, and you are irritated because you think they did a crappy job for which you paid good money. Your money is good money regardless of how much you paid for the services. Whether it is a $50 job or a $5,000 job, you should get what you paid for. It doesn't matter if this was a guy you found on Craigslist or a highly-rated professional. You paid someone to do a job, and they didn't hold up their end of the bargain. That's irritating.

But here's the thing: you catch more bees with honey than vinegar. Anyone who tries to be tactful understands this. You can be irate and angry in your tone, but that does not get people moving. Be understanding. Try to build something. Try to understand their viewpoint and get them to do something for you – not for their sake, necessarily, but for your own. Do it because it is the most effective way to get what you want done.

If they 'screwed' you, then you can save that situation, or you can tank it. I don't know about you, but I prefer saving things to making them worse. Not everyone is tactful, though, so they tank it – which, honestly, is what I used to do before I learned better. Five years ago, I was very abrasive. I'm sure I just shut a lot of people down. I had to learn how to talk to people to get them to do what I wanted them to do.

In this business, I deal with contractors who are mostly older men who nearly always think they know everything. They do know a lot, but their attitude tends to be that they know more than they actually do and their knowledge is irrefutable. It irks me a little bit, ok, a *lot*, but I get past it to save the situation.

There are two things you can do. First, take pictures of anything that has not been completed properly. Immediately jump to upper management or the owners of the company. A well-placed email with a picture of what you are dissatisfied with gets a very strong result. I do that immediately with zero emotion. I suggest you cut straight to the chase too.

Last weekend, I had some folks working on a house of mine. I was told the work was done, and I went out to the house to inspect the results. There was trash everywhere, and I took pictures. I escalated the situation immediately by sending an email to the owner of the company with a picture of the mess in my back room. I said, "Please schedule someone to pick up this mess. Photos attached." That's it. That's all I said. No threats, no opening, no closing. Simple, direct, and to the point. Was I irritated and mad? Absolutely. Did that come across? Of course. Did I cuss them out and yell? No. Did I cop an attitude and go on a rant? No. Did they come back and clean it up? Yes. They were way nice about it and even fixed a few extra things to keep me happy. They wanted a good review and my future business.

The reason I share this is because I am a natural warrior. My first instinct is FIGHT! not Love. So, I am showing what I have navigated to go from FIGHT to let's talk about this first before I threaten to sue. Everyone is different, but for the warriors out there – this is for you!

You'll find that with smaller companies it is easy to reach the owner or CEO. This isn't Target or Home Depot where you have layers of management. Do your research and figure out who it is you are talking to. A few houses ago, I had these guys installing my gutters, which is a part of my waterproofing. I was promised the job would be done in six to eight weeks. After three months, it still wasn't done (it wasn't critical). I kept calling the guy the salesperson told me was the head supervisor, and I never got anywhere. I left a bad review for them on Angie's List and immediately got a call from the owner asking why I didn't call him when things went south. He was livid that his employees had acted in this way and tarnished the name of his business. After speaking with him I realized that if I had done my own research to find out who he was and called him, I am sure things would have been resolved quickly and effectively.

You can be mad if you want. That's normal and natural. I don't want to have to tell a contractor to do their job right. They should do it correctly without me getting involved. Isn't that why you're paying them? But yelling at them, cursing at them, or making threats isn't going to help the situation. The contractor-investor relationship is NUANCED – that's why I want you to read this first, and understand your place – we need them, they need you, but if you have already paid them money, you don't want them to quit in the middle and lose your investment.

Make sure you handle disagreements in a way so they won't just hang up on you and not help you. Yell and scream at your cat, punch a pillow, complain to your friends, but don't do these things to or in front of the actual offender. Not because he doesn't deserve it, but because it will just make things worse. Your goal is to resolve the situation. Keep that goal in mind, and don't let your anger sabotage it.

The second trick is to be clear about what you want. Don't just say, "I don't like the way you did those gutters." Say, "You need to extend the gutters at least another six inches from the house." Take pictures and indicate on them what exactly is wrong with what has been done. A picture is worth a thousand words. The more specific you can be, the more likely you are to get what you want. "Move that thingie a little more towards the other doodad" might or might not get you any useful results. "Move the security light eight inches closer to the door frame" is more likely to get the security light where you want it to be. Be clear, as clarity will get you exactly what you want most times.

They might not do what you are asking them to do, but the more specific you are the more likely you are to get what you want. And remember – when you leave a picture with your review, it speaks volumes. Be sure to look at the pictures when you read reviews. Some people are more fastidious in their tastes – what seems horrible and shoddy to them may simply be 'not 100% perfect but still acceptable' to you. Or vice versa – someone may rave about something that looks slipshod to you. That's the reality of an online world. The company will tell you everything that is wonderful about them, but I want to know the truth, and the pictures will tell the truth.

In the end, though, if a company does not want to fix what they've done, they won't fix it, and there is very little you can do. In most cases, I take the hit and move on. I leave a negative, detailed review with pictures. I might register a complaint with the Better Business Bureau in the area. I rarely bother with court because it is expensive and it is very time consuming. Doing a cost-benefit analysis, I find that it is rarely worth my time. But you must do that analysis for yourself; that's a personal decision. If you are retired and don't have anything else to do, you might want to spend a day in the courthouse. I don't. That's my choice. It doesn't have to be your choice.

Usually, the worst-case scenario is that I am irritated, I take a small financial hit, and I move on. But I know I am leaving a public trail about how they act. People like me read these reviews and it matters in the long run. I've made a public mark. People can get a good look at who they are dealing with.

If it is a five-star, legitimate company that has an interest in the future, they will do what they need to do to fix the problem. The owner of a company who has a stake in the continuing business does not want its public reputation dragged through the mud. They do not want bad reviews. Escalate it quickly to resolve it quickly. Learn to use these words: "I am not happy with this level of service." Or, "I am not happy with this. I thought this would be better." You cannot force anyone to do what you want. If you keep this in mind and proceed accordingly, you can probably get them to *want* to do what you want, and then they will actually do it.

For women, sometimes it is a little harder because of the way we are conditioned to communicate. It is hard for us to be direct about how dissatisfied we are. We don't like being blunt, and we don't like hurting people's feelings. However, if you are nervous about it, try this trick: take the emotion out of it. Stick to facts, and be clear about what it *is*, not how you feel about it. Honestly, people appreciate that, especially men, and the majority of people you are dealing with in the construction industry are going to be men.

I learned this from a mentor I had in the corporate world. I was assigned to a project with a horrible project manager. He was the worst technical lead ever, and things were not getting done. My mentor kept asking me about it, and I was hedging. "Well, I mean, he's ok, but, it would be better if......" After way too much annoying hemming and hawing, my mentor stopped me and told me to just be clear and not worry about what the project manager thought about what I was saying. I took a deep breath and decided to be honest. I said, "Well, he's rude, abrasive, and obnoxious. I can't figure out what he wants me to do, and I have no idea what I did to get stuck on this project." My mentor just laughed and said that he knew that about this project manager. He said now that he knew how I felt we could work on what to do about it.

It was clear that I was so worried about trying to be nice and not burn any bridges that I wasn't being effective. Sometimes fire is destructive, and sometimes fire is cleansing. The male mind works that way – they prefer clear, precise, direct communication. Indirect communication tends to be confusing to most men. The clearer you are, the better the results. You're not trying to break them down or insult them or their work – you're just trying to tell them what you want.

Now that I think about it, that's good relationship advice, too.

Summary

- Take pictures and use them everywhere and anywhere you need to make your point

- Escalate quickly and go immediately to the top

- Be clear and direct

- Recognize that they may not do what you want them to do

- Leave reviews, both negative and positive, to encourage good work and to help other consumers who come after you

- Make sure the estimate is detailed, and that contract is set up to pay in three "draws" or parts as they complete each part in its entirety as the price of the total renovation increases (10k, 20k, 30k+).

SUCCESS STORY #7

My client, Christina, inherited a house from her grandmother. It was a small house, and it was paid for, and she was able to rent it out for a decent amount of money. She wasn't getting rich off it, but it put a few hundred dollars in her pocket every month. She saw the other houses in the neighborhood and knew that if she could snap up a few of them, she could put together a pretty tidy sum for herself.

The problem was that her grandmother's house was in another state and needed to have some significant upgrades. The uncertainty was scary. If she invested more money, would it be worth it or would she be throwing good money down the drain? The tenant in the house called her every time anything went wrong, and she had to take breaks from lunch to handle it. Being so far away she never felt comfortable with the time it took or the help she was trying to get. Small things like changing the air conditioner filter and popping a wayward screen back in were the extent of her problems. She was spending hours on a $5 fix and didn't know how to change this.

I worked with Christina on putting together a team. She was doing too much by herself! We found a property manager that could run out and do the small fixes and a team of contractors that could do the larger ones. She soon figured out that she didn't have to be doing all the work she was doing. Once she stopped spending her time trying to be a Jackie-of-All-Trades and let the experts do their business, she found she had plenty of time to amass more properties and sit back as the checks rolled in.

CHAPTER 9

Investing Out of State

There are a lot of reasons why you might choose to invest out of state. It may be that the area in which you live doesn't have the right kinds of properties for you to invest in (or in your budget). You may be planning for the future and want to set up your investment business where you expect to retire. You might be buying houses near where your children are attending college, or you may have family in the area. It doesn't really matter why. The point is that with this system, you can easily set up your real estate investing business far from home without too much trouble.

The key is your team. A good team can manage the day-to-day aspects of the business for you. They can handle repairs and tenant concerns without you being physically present. Ideally, your team runs so smoothly that you can sit at a distance answering emails and phone calls from time to time and that's it.

Life isn't ideal, however, and you are going to need to visit the property occasionally. So, when you are choosing to invest out of state, make sure that this is something you will be able to do when it is necessary. If your work schedule or financial constraints are too tight, or if you have some other condition in your life that prevents travel, it may ultimately be a problem.

What exactly do we mean when we talk about investing out of state? 'Out of state' can mean a lot of different things to a lot of different people. Depending on where you live, out of state can mean ten minutes down the road or a considerable distance from where you are. Whether it is close or far, there are still some similar considerations. There are additional things to think about if you choose to invest in a different region of the country. You may be able to drive the distance, or you may have to fly. There may be alternative transportation like trains and buses available, or there may not. There may not be an airport within an hour or two of the property, necessitating car rentals and other transportation concerns if you have to fly there.

Where you are (point A) and where the potential property is (point B) can make a big difference. Sometimes it is cheap to fly from one city to another, and there are a lot of flights available to accommodate the different times of day you may need to go. Some cities are more difficult to access. You may have to transfer planes, and flights may not be at convenient times. The flights might always be expensive. Don't just assume that you can just get from anywhere to anywhere at any time. That isn't always true. Some cities, like Atlanta, are major airport hubs and you can almost always find a flight in or out. Other cities, like Chicago, might be more difficult.

When you have to fly out of state, like my California clients who want to build a modest portfolio do– we don't decide on a market until we know:

1. Travel time and costs

2. How many reputable property management companies are available to manage their rentals (my minimum is four for my out of state clients)

3. Can your schedule account for flying out of town to visit every other week at least the first couple of months (this will vary, but it's best to be prepared)

Let's go over these in detail and discuss how you should make different investment decisions depending on your situation.

1. Travel Time and Costs

Unless you are a long-haul trucker, anything more than two hours driving time in one direction is going to be too much. If it's three hours (do not go to four hours driving time each way), I only let me clients go if they clearly understand they should stay overnight in a hotel or Airbnb, as six hours' round trip in a day is very burdensome when you add managing some part of a renovation. So, less than two hours for driving.

For those who are flying, I do not recommend a more than two-hour flight time. Check your local airport, and find the flight routes and daily flights for the top five airlines. If you have a choice of five cities, the one that has daily flights priced at $125 round trip on any day of the week (especially Saturday) is an excellent market to look for rentals compared to one that is 3.5 hours away, has a layover, and flights range from $300-$350 for round trip tickets.

One client I had lived outside of Baltimore, MD and decided that Pittsburgh was going to be his market – it's $125 round trip on Southwest Airlines, and less than a two-hour flight. And he likes Pittsburgh (it's a fun city). As a single woman, I usually do what I need to do, and I am safely in my hotel/Airbnb suite by dark, which is my comfort level when traveling on my own. You see how when you take those items into account, investing out of state can be amazing and quite easy?

2. *Reputable Property Management Companies That Service Your Area*

If you are investing long distance, one of the first factors that will determine if you will invest there is the number of property management companies in the area. Select at least four companies with good reputations that service the neighborhoods in which you want to invest. I always say – before investing out of state, know that the property will be properly managed by choosing a market that can support being a rental property owner versus a landlord.

I mentioned earlier that property management companies can go wrong. In Baltimore, the two property management companies I hired still owe me small amounts of money ($250 for one, $480 on the other). To this day, I have not received the money, and it's not worth going taking them to court. And, it was challenging finding another management company that had a GOOD reputation (there are a lot out of there, but good ones? In my opinion, they get overburdened very quickly and don't know how to scale with the increased demand in this location).

Another example is my Columbus, OH rental. I had to fire my first management company for not communicating well and not managing rent collection well (its two main jobs). They were barely passable, but no communication and I didn't receive my rent. I fired them and hired another company that lasted three years. I had to let them go because they ran things well, but their costs to turn over a unit was $3000, which was double what it

[handwritten margin note: Having multiple property managers in the area allows for a lot/would broaden things to look]

should have been (They were based in Cincinnati, and their contractors were in Columbus, so they paid the premium to some contractors instead of finding better ones). So, I am on my third property manager in eight years. They are great, up-to-date, and I like them. But you see how having a minimum of four property management companies ensures I can hold onto my rental? If I had known and checked in Baltimore, I would have avoided investing there. Now I am selling in Baltimore so I can invest in the Virginia market. That's how big a deal property management companies are, and why you should absolutely make sure you have multiple choices so you can switch if it's not working out (which can happen for a variety of reasons)

3. Your Schedule

For most of us, we are investing in real estate while still working a full-time job. TAKE THAT INTO ACCOUNT! If you are a father or mother with kids, who can't just take off to see a property – then maybe this isn't for you now. But what if you can put kid tunes on in the car and take the kids with you as you travel? Then you're onto something.

I had a client in New York who decided to invest in North Carolina. She got in the car and drove 5.5 hours there, with her two kids (that's longer than I would recommend for any of my clients, but she had family out there and was okay with it). She made it happen and she is excited, but not everyone can travel like that. If you cannot, we may need to look at increasing your budget and find something that you can work with locally that doesn't need a lot of work.

If your weekends are full and your plans are not flexible, you really need to understand that; and it's not all doom and gloom.

I've worked with nurses who have Thursday – Sunday off. I've worked with flight attendants who fly all the time, so flying from Texas to Oklahoma for a rental was easy to do. I also have worked with engineers, IT specialists, Government Contractors in DC, and housewives in Utah and Massachusetts. Guess what? You need to have a discussion of how much time they have available to take off to invest, or just to look for properties, and consider that when looking for property locations.

The full-time workers with kids who also runs a church – he had two hours a week. You can get something if you have the time available, but it won't necessarily be a great deal (those will be taken by the time you are available to look and find a great rental). And don't worry about that preacher – he will have his time, but for right now it's not looking so easy.

Those are the main concerns, and if you take them into account, investing out of state is fun and easy when you account and navigate with your lifestyle.

Remember: Sometimes we have to make sacrifices when we want to build a portfolio of our dreams. However, I would rather you know the sacrifices you need to take BEFORE you invest 10-20k in a property. So, if your travel time is longer but you really love the market, deal, location, etc., at least you are completely aware of your options before making that decision to invest.

I recommend documenting these factors on an Excel spreadsheet to keep track of your options as you determine which market you will decide on.

4. *Other concerns to navigate as you are deciding on your market.*

Depending upon your preferences, transportation within the city you choose and its surrounding areas (where your properties are likely to be located) may vary widely. Some cities have extensive public transportation systems. When you go to those cities, you might be able to get around cheaply and easily without having to rent a car. Other cities aren't so easy to get around, and you will have to factor in the cost of renting a car, taxis, or Uber into your travel budget.

If you are traveling, you also need to consider where you are going to stay. Some neighborhoods don't have hotels in them, and AirBNB-type properties might be non-existent. If you will have to stay 10-20 miles away from the property, that might be prohibitive.

Much of this depends on your standards – some people will only sleep in a Marriott or better, and some people just need a clean place to lay their head. If you insist on room service availability and a Starbucks within walking distance, you're not likely to find a hotel with those amenities in a working-class neighborhood. If you don't mind gas station coffee and a pre-wrapped muffin for breakfast, you may have more options near the property.

In the beginning, when you are setting up your team, you may need to be present more often. I tell my coaching clients to budget for flying out once every two to three weeks during the first two months. I have my California clients make a $2,000 travel budget just for this.

But remember, if you consider travel time and cost, even your available travel schedule, this should fit right into your current lifestyle.

There's something about looking someone directly in the eye and seeing what's behind there that can't be done over the telephone or by Skype. You're going to want to talk to your team members in person and shake their hands. Your team should match your goal. You don't want to hire property managers for homes in working-class neighborhoods that are going to roll up in a Mercedes wearing $400 shoes. They may be able to talk a good game, but until you get a look at them, you won't know if they're a good fit for the types of properties you're trying to invest in. And they might not be comfortable themselves in less well-kept neighborhoods.

This is why a property management company is so important – you will rely heavily on them to give you updates on the contractors (use a simple lockbox system, and let them know to send pics of completed work and change the code when you're not there). Here's where their boots on the ground knowledge is invaluable. You should have a conversation with your property management about them overseeing the project – most property management companies will stop by your renovation and ensure it is moving along, usually for a set fee in the contract. They are part of the reason this system works, so you don't have to fly into town every weekend. Once the property is up and running, you only need to visit one to two times a year, as you feel comfortable.

I've only invested out of state. It's as easy for me to invest non-locally as it is for others to invest across the street. We've figured out what's necessary and what's not necessary, and in less time; but once it's up and running, which I help my clients do and scale, you don't have to go back. I have three properties I did not visit in for a three- to six-year period, and they are just fine. I know everything that happens. I get pictures upon move in, upon move out, and in between. I know the story of who lives there and gave final approval. I can visit, but I'm superfluous at this point as I already made sure the systems are in place. They are doing great, by the way!

There's no substitute for been-there-done-that information given to you by someone without a dog in the fight to cloud their judgment. If you can find someone who has connections in that particular area, you've found a tremendous resource you need to leverage. Property Managers are great, and if you need to, going to a local Real Estate Investor Association (REIA) is great for word-of-mouth networking as well. If you can, make sure to schedule your trip to coordinate with a local REIA and stay an extra day if needed.

Even though I can do most of the groundwork online using the CPR Technique I outlined earlier, I wouldn't ever buy a property sight unseen.

I repeat. Do not purchase a property sight unseen.

There are wholesalers everywhere trying to get rid of properties. Don't take the bait! A real estate agent may have several pictures of a wonderful looking house and forgot to include the picture of the crumbling foundation, or the giant crack in the wall. This happens. My coaching clients and I have found that about 50% of the homes that look good on paper look horrible in person. Don't take that chance. Schedule time to look.

Virtual seeing isn't enough for me to invest my money. I want to see it. I want to know that there isn't some train that runs through every thirty minutes and makes a racket. I want to see with my own eyes that the stains on the wall can be covered with paint and aren't from water damage. I want to make sure that I can't smell the pork rendering plant a few miles down the road or the garbage dump not too far away. You can't get the real 'feel' of a place without visiting it personally. You can't see who is hanging out on the street corner or who the neighbors will be. Only when I am there do I get that sense in my gut about whether the property is right. Online I can tell if it is a possibility, but in person is when I know for sure.

Evictions, Inspections, Move-in, Move-out, Court Cases

Unless you're suing your Property Management companies, you don't have to worry about traveling there. It's a lot easier to do than you think when you take your time and know what's important and what advice you can throw away. The advice in this book is important.

Don't assume that everything is the same from state to state. Although federal housing laws apply across the entire United States, each state – and each county, town, city, parish, or political subdivision – may have its own rules that you need to be aware of. If you own the properties through your corporation or business, you may need to register that business with the local Secretary of State's office as a foreign entity. In Baltimore, as part of the eviction process, they check to see you are fully registered to be a rental (and ensure you have paid all the fees you were supposed to pay). The standard lease that you use may need to be adjusted to reflect local zoning laws and tenant protection laws. It's always a good idea to get a state-specific lease and ask your property management company about their experience obtaining a successful eviction. Eviction procedures may be completely different. Your local team can help you navigate these potential pitfalls.

The laws protecting tenants are something you should be especially wary of. I'm not saying that there shouldn't be laws protecting tenants from unscrupulous landlords, but if someone is not paying you rent or is damaging your property, you should be able to protect yourself. Some places have laws that are so cumbersome that it is a time consuming, lengthy, and difficult process to get rid of someone who isn't paying. It changes from city to city, so have a quick conversation with a Property Management company, or join an online forum, and inquire how landlord or tenant friendly that place is. How long it takes and how much it costs should give you an indication. Baltimore and New York can be three to six months, but Atlanta and Richmond are 30 days to six weeks. These are major differences and should be considered before deciding on what market you want to build your rental portfolio in.

Remember, as I discussed above, you don't buy the property first and *then* find your team. The team comes first. I cannot overemphasize the importance of getting your team in place on the front end enough, especially if you are going to be an absentee landlord and live somewhere else. Your team needs to be on the ball, trustworthy, and responsive. If they aren't, you may find yourself holding the bag, and the bag might have fines and other assessments and troubles in it. That's why you find the team *first* – how else will you know you can even find a team?

Calling All Nurses

Glynnis was a full-time nurse who I took on as a coaching client. She lived in California with her husband and had a good amount saved up, but Southern California is a great place to work and save money, but not to buy property.

After a week in the program (it goes fast now), we found the perfect market in the Midwest for her. Not only were round-trip tickets for FRIDAY – SUNDAY travel $150 on Frontier Airlines, but her husband also loved this part of Missouri because of the historical museums. They both enjoyed visiting their investment AND their family. They met the friendliest agent who would drive around to properties for them and introduced them to wonderful contractors. They found a duplex for $110,000 (my clients average about $70,000 for duplexes, so this was higher, but worth it), and needed very little work to earn $1600 a month in rent. They couldn't even find a property in this price range in California. Their cash flow was great, and with it being multi-family (which I insist upon for my Californians), if one side goes empty, the mortgage and then some is still covered. She's happy, her husband is happy, her family is happy they get to see her – everyone is happy. That's the power of knowing how to navigate out of state rental property ownership. She doesn't have to wait until she's 70 and has a ton of money in the bank. She can start modestly today. Everyone is different, though, so you should find the market that works for you.

CHAPTER 10

Your Business Has To Be a *Business*

What does it mean to be a business? Does it mean making money? Does it mean engaging in transactions with other people? What, if any, is the difference between a corporation and a business?

Business is a general term. It can mean anything from a lemonade stand to a blue-chip-been-around-forever-and-will-be-around-forever-international-company like Coca-Cola or my old employer, IBM. It is anything that provides a good (a product, a thing, something you can touch or take) or a service (like a haircut or doing your tax return) in exchange for something of value.

A corporation is something more specific. It is a government-defined entity. Depending on which state you live in (assuming you live in the United States,) there will be a particular set of rules and procedures about how to set up a corporation. While the details may vary, the generalities are the same.

A corporation is its own thing. You've probably heard the phrase "corporate personhood" in the news. While the details of what that means are too off topic for this book, it's a good idea to keep in mind that when you are creating a company, you are essentially creating a 'person.' A fake person, but a person with its own social security number[9], debts, and income. The main advantage of having a corporation to own your properties is to limit your liability, maximize your tax savings, and to avoid being audited.

Contrary to popular belief, you do NOT need to put your house in your LLC or business entity. First, you can't get a mortgage and will have to purchasing using all cash. Second, it makes it difficult to get the equity out, because you will have to transfer ownership into your name if you want to refinance. A better way to protect your assets is to establish a parent company, then establish a child company like a financing LLC. The sole purpose of that company is equity stripping. Meaning, if the building is worth $70,000 and you owe $60,000, it's not a target since it doesn't have much equity in the case of a lawsuit. However, if it's worth $70,000 and you own it free and clear – now you will have to worry about the equity that's just sitting there. At that point, you will look to place a mechanic's lien through your financing LLC against the property so the equity is stripped. Of course, you need to look at the cost of filing liens, and what liens are available, but that's a much better solution. More of this in detail can be seen in my full year access to *Investing Made Easy Full Year Access* (look under Ebere Okoye Accounting Sessions) or *Best of Ask the Professionals* series.

There really isn't a disadvantage. You should talk to an accountant or lawyer about which is best for you, but an LLC,[10] LLP, or an S-Corp[11] are what are called "pass-through"

---

[9] Known as an EIN (Employer's Identification Number) or a TIN (Tax-payer's Identification Number)
[10] Limited Liability Company
[11] Limited Liability Partnership

corporations. This means that they don't pay their own taxes, their profit or loss goes on to your (the owner's) tax returns. Otherwise, you'd be paying taxes twice on the income, and that wouldn't be good. You can pay yourself a salary or a portion of the profits as 'dividends.' Which one you chose, and how you choose to do it, is something to talk to an accountant about since there are tax consequences for each.

Also, multi-member LLC, LLPs, and S-Corps get audited at a rate of 0.4% – the least of any entities.

Setting up the corporation isn't necessarily difficult. You can go to your Secretary of State website (i.e., Google *Virginia Secretary of State Business Entity* and you'll see your filing paper to fill out and the filing fee). But as far as protection, and how to structure the operating agreement so you don't run afoul of the IRS, a savvy real estate investing accountant can help with that. My favorite real estate investing accountant is Ebere Okoye, the Wealth Building CPA. She's wonderful and gained her experience by working with the largest real estate investor in DC. That's big money and influence right there, and she was a part of it at the beginning of her career. She will show you how to structure your parent company so that ordinary and necessary business expenses can be deducted, not just one the first day you place your rental in service. She's amazing. If you go to her, tell her you heard about her from her from affordable real estate investments (You can find her here – The Wealth Building CPA – www.TheWealthBuildingCPA.com) – the more business she gets, the more willing she is to attend our 3-day investing intensives so you get to ask her these questions live!

---

[12] Referring to Section "S" of the IRS Code

This is especially true if you have a business partner. Everything is easy when things are going well, but even the best of partnerships eventually will have a dispute. When that occurs, you want to make sure that you have a good partnership agreement that addresses what to do. For example, what if you want to pull money out of the business, but your business partner wants to use that money to invest in another house? How do you decide who wins the argument? A good partnership will have clearly-defined roles for each person. Or what happens if your partner wants to get out of the business and sell it to his cousin? Do you have to do business with your partner's cousin? What happens if one of you dies? What happens if one of you gets sick and can't do any of the work – do you still split the money evenly? You need to discuss this, and come up with a solution that works – don't stick your head in the sand. My partnership agreement will look different than your agreement – because we are different people with varying finances, priorities and talents that we bring. Reach a conclusion you feel happy about, but make sure it's addressed before more money and time is invested.

Even if you are on your own, a well-defined corporate structure can help protect you from liability and tax consequences and make it possible to get business credit. Banks may require certain corporate documents to give you loans in a corporate name without a personal guarantee. Most lawyers will not charge much to help you set it up correctly to avoid headaches down the line.

ACCOUNTING AND BOOKKEEPING

As I mentioned earlier, I'm trained as an engineer. Math and numbers have always been my strong suit. I recognize that's not true for everyone, or even for most people. Still, no matter how

Make sure partnership agreements are in place before investing starts

good or bad at math you are, it's important that you keep good financial records.

I've worked with a lot of people who panic when they get to this part of the business. Some people keep a shoebox full of receipts and figure their accountant will deal with it at the end of the year. Some people don't even do that, and think if there is money in the checking account they are doing ok. THIS IS NOT TRUE!!!

I cannot stress this enough. I've seen more than one great business go under because of poor accounting.

Bookkeeping and Accounting are art forms and skills, and you don't have to be good at them to make this work. There are several computer programs that you can use that will make it easy, like *QuickBooks Self Employed* for $5 per month. It's the least expensive online accounting software and makes year-end tax time and estimated taxes simple. When I have a receipt, I can snap a picture of it directly and toss the receipt. Love it! You can then reference these records if you need to find them for your accountant, the IRS, or if you need to show that you paid for something for a lawsuit or other claim. If you can't figure out how to set up your books or your computer program, you can hire someone to set it up for you and teach you how to use it on your own. Or, it might be worth your while to hire a bookkeeper to keep track of things for you. Don't fall into the trap of thinking that just because there is money in the bank account that there is money available for you to use for yourself.

Getting a tax deduction with all these expenses is an art form itself, and involves structuring this properly. Technically, as a landlord, you are not supposed to deduct any expense on your property until the first day its placed in service. But what about all the travel, training, and other expenses for repair and maintenance? That's why having a parent company that specifies continuing training/education and travel are ordinary and necessary expenses, as well as other items, then you can deduct costs associated with running your business, regardless of the date your unit is placed in service. There is a lot more nuance to this of course, so in order to not get into trouble, I suggest you watch the accountants speaking (again, I love Ebere Okeye's sessions) which is why I recommend you look into *Investing Made Easy Full Year Access* (look under Ebere Okeye Accounting Sessions) or *Best of Ask the Professionals* series.

Commingling of Funds

The phrase "Commingling of Funds" sounds criminal, but it really isn't. It is more of a bad idea than something nefarious. It can get you into some serious financial trouble as far as separating your assets, and potentially run you aground with the IRS.

Commingling of funds means putting funds from two or more different sources or purposes together. In this case, I'm talking about your business money and your personal money. KEEP THEM SEPARATE. Also, if you have a business checking account, you can apply to that bank for a business credit card that you can use forever, so it's another major reason to have a business entity. (The business credit card reports to commercial credit bureaus, not consumer credit bureaus so it won't show up on your credit report. This alone is worth it!)

It is easy to fall into the trap of using one checkbook or debit card for everything. Don't do it! As complicated and confusing as accounting and bookkeeping can be, it is even more so when you are paying for your personal Netflix Account or your shopping spree at T.J. Maxx with your business Visa card. If you go to Target or Wal-Mart to buy cleaning supplies to clean up one of your properties, and while you are there you pick up a new toaster oven for your personal house, you should pay for those things with two different credit cards (your business card and your personal card) in two different transactions and get two different receipts. If you deduct your personal items as a business expense, that's technically tax fraud. It's a nightmare to try to separate expenses out on a crumpled receipt and figure out what portion of the tax goes with what item.

It's a simple rule: things for your business go with your business accounts. Things for your personal life go with your personal accounts. Make sure if you do have multiple items on your receipt, you circle and initial the business items and file the receipt.

Budgeting and Money Management

The biggest part of accounting is knowing what you have. Knowing what you have is important, but so is knowing what you need. How can you figure out what you are going to need, especially when you are first starting out?

This is one of the many times when having a good mentor is helpful, especially one that can hook you up with mentoring groups that consist of investors like you who are in various stages of their investment journey. People who have "been there and done that" are your best way to gauge what you are going to need.

There is no number that I can just give you here. Much of that is geographical. Things cost more or less depending on where in the country you are. Some things, like air conditioning units in the deep south, wear out more often than in other parts of the country. Some parts of the country have floods every few years and some parts never do. Talk to people who have experience where you are. Estimate the amount you need to set aside for taxes, insurance, and repairs, and make sure that you keep that amount available. You may be comfortable keeping that amount available in an equity line of credit, or you may be more comfortable keeping it in a savings account. Your property management company may require you to keep a certain amount on hand for them to draw from for minor repairs. Which method works for you is somewhat personal. You should talk with your mentor and your mentoring group to feel out the advantages and disadvantages. In Chapter 4 – "Cash Flow Analysis," we put away about 15% a month for incidental maintenance and vacancy expenses as a good rule of thumb. It has served me well in these last nine years. I fully renovated those homes when I moved tenants in, so they are all in like-new condition and I only get occasional maintenance calls.

The important thing is not what form those funds are in, but rather that you have access to those funds when you need them. When your tenant calls to tell you that the water heater has gone out and it is below freezing outside –- and they will! (most likely at the worst possible time – you can do something about it right away without worrying about where the money is going to come from. That peace of mind is priceless and well worth resisting the temptation to spend every bit of money that comes into your account.

CHAPTER 11

Choosing a Mentor

I've referenced mentors a few times in this book, and I cannot stress enough how important they are to your investment business. There are a lot of folks out there who are willing to mentor you and give you advice. How do you know which one is right for you?

Instinct is huge for me. I'm a very intuitive person, and I think most people are taught to ignore their intuition to their detriment. We are told repeatedly to use facts and figures only and ignore what our gut tells us. This is well-meaning advice, but it isn't good advice. If it feels right, it probably is. Listen to that inner voice. She's telling you the truth! She's noticing the things your conscious mind is not able to process. While your brain is processing facts and figures, your subconscious voice is noting passion and honesty and a true sense of value.

It's important that your mentor's tactics line up with your pocketbook. If you read an article about someone who went from 0 to 80 units in six months – is that something you can do (or want to do)? Did they do that by having $200,000 to put down, and were able to raise $500,000 through friends and family? If yes, you should understand that model needs to be practical for you. My friends and social acquaintances are first-generation college-educated African Americans. We had to pay our student loans, get a job, learn about credit the hard way, and still maintain a certain lifestyle. So, asking someone for 50k isn't possible for me or the majority of my social circle.

However, my sister-in-law is from a family where her two brothers asked their father for a $120,000 loan to open a couple of KFC franchises – and got it.

If you come from my line and the most you can get from your parents is 5k, you need to make sure you are taking advice from a mentor that comes from the same place you do financially. I have emails from people who followed the advice and have an "A class" loser that's underwater because that advice is for people who can wait around 20-30 years to pay off a $250,000 loan. That's what listening to someone who's pocketbook does not align with your reality can do to you.

Their values need to line up with your own. If you're all about money, money, money, then find a mentor that makes you see dollar signs and doesn't care about anything else. If you're about empowering African American professionals to create independence through investing in underserved neighborhoods, about giving hardworking people and families a great place to live while making money at the same time – like me - then find a mentor who shares that passion and find strategies for your pocketbook that resonate with their methods.

For the most part, mentors are not going to be free. Mentors are successful in their field, and they are willing and able to impart their experience to people who share their vision and goals. But their time is valuable, and they have demands made on them, so you need to pay them for their time. You aren't paying them for something you can touch. You are paying them for their knowledge. Just like you pay tuition to a college to get knowledge from the professors, you pay your mentor to get knowledge from the wealth of experience they have. There's nothing wrong or shady about that.

Unlike colleges, however, there is no accreditation system or high school guidance counselor to point you in the right direction. You have to do your research. So how do you do that?

The internet is a great place to start. YouTube has thousands of videos of people giving away information that can get you started. My YouTube channel can be found at YouTube.com/user/AffordableREI – go ahead and look and join the 16,000+ current subscribers. You can download a free training bundle, and hear my voice, and see if I speak to you in a way that resonates with you. Honestly, I don't want to take people's money until I know they are going to be comfortable with me. If we don't share the same passion, if it isn't a good fit, there's no reason we should be wasting our time with each other. I'm sure most ethical mentors feel the same way.

Another thing I do to make people comfortable with me is conduct workshops around the country. Last year, I went to Miami, Atlanta, New York, and Las Vegas, among other places. These workshops are great! You can meet other like-minded investors, and listen to me and other successful people in the industry. For people who are more visual and tangible, they can get a better sense this way of how they feel. I don't believe in playing hide the ball. And, it doesn't hurt that it is fully catered from cocktails to dinner (I like to give the full luxury experience). Find out more about my live events here (Or get the free training bundle – Lisa-Phillips.thinkific.com/courses/my-live-events/)

Make mentor fit to you

You want to make sure that you find a mentor that is willing to meet you where you are. Too many people try to stuff you into a one-size-fits-all box. More like one-size-fits-none! We're all individuals with our own histories, starting points, and goals. Your mentor should recognize that and take the time to get to know you and where you are coming from. I like talking to my mentees and watching their dreams take shape. It wouldn't be half as much fun imposing my dreams on them. I've already formed the investment business I want for me. Now it is time for YOU to create the investment business YOU want for YOU. Just like all the clothes in your closet aren't going to fit me as perfectly as they fit you, your dreams aren't going to fit me as perfectly as they fit you. Make sure you find the kind of mentor that recognizes that.

I like to be flexible. It's not my way or the highway. I have what feels like a million different mentoring programs – one to suit every type of person. We will find a program that works for you, even if we have to make one up. Some people prefer to watch videos on their own time and then ask questions when. Some people prefer more one-on-one time. Some people like the groups more. I offer all kinds of combinations of services. I'm not going to try to stuff you into a size six petite when you're really a size 14. You are who you are, and I'm going to give you what you need. You can look good at any size and shape.

Mentorship is building a relationship. It's not *like* building a relationship; it *is* building a relationship. Think of it this way: when you're a kid, your Mom finances everything and teaches you what you need to know. Once you're on your own, your relationship with Mom isn't financial anymore, but the lessons you learned from her are still part of your life. That's why I give access to my exclusive online courses to my mentees for life.

Once you're in, you're in. You'll eventually leave the nest, but you'll still be a part of my family.

It makes me sad to think that there are people out there who just want to take your money, but there are. You can't get extra time with them, they don't deliver their all to make sure you understand every decision you're making and how it will affect your finances and portfolio. Sometimes they just don't know, other times they are money hungry and want you to pay for more, so nothing is included. It's hard to watch. I've had people come to me who are skeptical and cynical and with good cause. They've paid good money to folks who have promised the moon and delivered not much more than the crumbs of a Moon Pie. It gives people like me a bad name, and I don't like that at all. That's why I give so much away on YouTube and at my workshops. I want you to see what you're going to get before you make an investment. I want you to be able to see and hear my drive and passion with your own eyes and ears before making a decision.

And most of all, I want you to listen to your heart and to what that inner voice says. Your instincts will lead you to the right place, I promise.

If you would like me to help you directly in building the best rental property strategy for you and get a **FREE 45 MINUTE STRATEGY SESSION to see if I can help you achieve your goals, visit:**

LisaPhillipsrei.clickfunnels.com/page-1ight7o0n

WORKING WITH A MENTOR - EXAMPLE PRIVATE CLIENT WORK

At Affordable Real Estate Investments, we start our private coaching with a strategy call. From there, we assess what may be stopping you from building a low-cost rental property portfolio, and determine what program is the best for you. Details are listed below if you want to skip the strategy session call.

We start off with a kick-off strategy session call with my Private 1-1 Clients within three days of signing them up and bringing them on board. In this important call, we figure out the client's unique strategy for building their rental property business. The strategy changes based on the client's current financial resources and credit profile, as well as their geographic location. We gather the information necessary to determine how to make this work with the client's work schedule, as well as guide them to the initial steps for analyzing what will be the best market for them.

From there, we analyze different markets, both local and long distance, to assess which ones meet all the unique criteria for them personally, as well as just great criteria needed to get the best deal for their investments. This includes determining everything from the type of neighborhoods the client feels comfortable investing in to the amount of travel time. This usually is accomplished within the first two weeks.

Once the perfect market for my client has been chosen, an earnest search will begin. The client will lead the way in selecting potential properties and together we will analyze each deal – usually the clients become more sophisticated with each round as they learn from previous analysis sessions. We do that together over the phone, as needed for the market. During this time, the client is asked to schedule a time to look at properties in person, be it within driving distance or out of state (cost and travel time have already been considered so that this isn't a hardship). This is within the next two to three weeks.

After their tour of the homes, we will analyze together which homes they should bid on and how much to bid using any associated pictures and videos. This usually takes a week.

Typically, back and forth bidding occurs until the seller agrees to the buyer's terms, and the closing process starts (for one home, and sometimes for two). At this time, we prepare for the inspection process, determine the next steps for contracting any repairs, discuss managing the property long distance, and begin the search for a tenant.

This entire process takes about 7-10 weeks depending on time availability, travel ability, and financial resources, and not ALL the details were included. I hope that any coaching relationship you undertake is as detailed and thoughtful as this can be for you. My Private 1-1 clients have an easy, exciting, and stress-free experience, and now know how to start maximizing their portfolios.

Investing should be easy, fun, and rewarding.

The following is a list of standalone trainings and coaching programs we offer. If one of them is the perfect fit for your goals and your budget, I hope to see you sign up!

Coaching

Affordable Real Estate Investments has 3-tier coaching support offerings. They are the **Sub30k Accelerator Program**, The **Black Diamonds Mastermind**, and **Private 1-1 coaching**.

Sub30k Accelerator Program

The Sub30k Accelerator Program has two Live calls per month, which is perfect for the beginning investor who is comfortable working on their own and is looking for an accountability team.

Black Diamonds Mastermind

The Black Diamonds Mastermind includes everything in the Accelerator Program PLUS weekly group coaching calls for the beginning investor who is ready to get started this month and is looking for more frequent support.

Private 1-1 Training

Private 1-1 coaching support includes full phone and email access, all training courses, and a 2.5-day intensive event, perfect for the beginning investor who is ready to get started today and would like an experienced professional to walk them through the entire process.

Learn more about these detailed and affordable coaching programs at AffordableRealEstateInvestments.com/training-center

Self–Paced Training

For those who would like to learn on their own at their own pace, our training center offers three different self-paced learning series to choose from: **Investing Made Easy Monthly Membership**, the **Sub30k Education Collection**, And the **Sub30k Rental Income System**.

Investing Made Easy Monthly Membership

If you want to learn how to get your rental property business set up the right way to protect your assets, bank account, and credit score, we have the Investing Made Easy Monthly Membership.

Sub30k Education Collection

If you would like gain more in-depth knowledge about the strategy of investing in lower-priced real estate properties (way more than I could include in one book), we offer the Sub30k Education Collection.

Sub30k Rental Income System

Finally, if you are the kind of person who wants to learn on your own at your own pace, we offer The Sub30k Rental Income System, which has all the step-by-step details on building a low-priced rental portfolio from A to Z.

These are easy to implement and affordable training modules with action steps and worksheets. To learn more, visit our training center:

AffordableRealestateInvestments.com/training-center

CHAPTER 12

Summary and Conclusion

I wish I could have written more, but I don't want to create a 500-page binder that you never read. So, I started with the most important metrics that keep my coaching clients successfully building excellent rental property portfolios, all around the country.

We've all seen those infomercials where some guy in a white linen suit is riding a speedboat, dripping with supermodels and gold chains, claiming he made his millions in real estate and he wants to teach you how he did it. Those schemes aren't for real people – they're pyramid schemes; they work for people whose families can give them 'small' loans of $1,000,000 to get started, or mostly they don't work at all. The infomercials paid a lot of money to be advertising, and they are looking for whales – 50k sign-up fee type whales.

You and I are not like that. We came from working-class neighborhoods. Our mothers and fathers wore uniforms or cleaned other people's houses and offices, they punched time clocks and worked the graveyard shift. We've worked hard all our lives just like them, and we expect to continue to work hard all our lives. We don't expect the easy life, but we want security. We want to know that we have a living income at all times so that we don't have to worry about where tomorrow's dinner will come from and whether there will be a solid roof over our heads. We want to know that no matter what the economy does, our cash flow will remain intact. And we want to be able to look at ourselves in the mirror and know that what we are doing is making the world a better place.

Affordable real estate investing, using my CPR Technique, checks all those boxes. It can give you a secure, passive, steady income. It can empower you to take control of your life in a world that sometimes seems beyond us. And it can allow you to provide decent, quality, affordable housing to hardworking, deserving families who need a safe place to live.

You can be a landlord without being the stereotypical slumlord, pulling up in a limousine to a falling down tenement with no heat in the winter demanding rent within 24 hours or you will toss poor old granny out on the street. You can be kind and generous and helpful – AND make a profit!

Even more exciting – you can do it without having a rich daddy to get you started or a fat slush fund to draw from with the tips and tricks I've talked about in this book, with only the most minimal of savings and questionable credit. I did it on the heels of a foreclosure, with no job, and with no family or friends loaning me money to start. If I can, you can. Especially with my help.

What are you waiting for? **LET'S START INVESTING!**

About the Author

LISA PHILLIPS has helped thousands of people follow their dreams and get instant cash flow through affordable real estate investing. Her easy-to-follow program guarantees success and security for those who want it.

Learn more about Lisa at AffordableRealEstateinvestments.com

Learn more about Lisa's Affordable Real Estate Investing Program at Lisa-Phillips.thinkific.com

Make sure to get a **FREE** copy of Investing in Rental Properties for Beginners Companion Course at Lisa-Phillips.thinkific.com/courses/investing-in-rental-properties-for-beginners-companion-course/

Join Lisa's Facebook Group here: Facebook.com/groups/Sub30kMastermindGroup

And like my Facebook page to connect and chat to me directly – Facebook.com/affordablerei

Can You Do Me a Favor?

My goal is to impact millions and help bridge the gap between poverty and prosperity for those who think financial freedom is only for the rich. And you can help be a part of that shift. So please, be a part of the bigger picture, and make sure people know they have options – and let them know they have a fair chance despite all the advice out there that makes them feel hopeless.

If you enjoyed this book or found it useful, I'd be very grateful if you'd post a short review on Amazon. Books like mine really help support the middle class, the working class – both as investors with modest pocketbooks and for who we are providing housing. And it works. And without your support, there are going to be so many more people who think they can't have the dream because they're not rich enough when they can!

You can help make sure this message gets through to everyone, and help those who lost hope know that they can build their financial freedom as well – no big pockets needed.

Be a part of the middle-class army that's learning how to take our time back, and our neighborhoods, and impact this country for the better.

Your support really does make a difference and I read all the reviews personally so I can get your feedback and make this book even better.

Make sure you grab my free *Investing in Rental Properties for Beginners Companion Course* and be treated like the kings and queens you are.

If you'd like to leave a review, then all you need to do is go to Amazon and pull up my book and write your review.

Thanks again for your support!

My Soul Powered Life

MY SOUL POWERED LIFE

ANYTHING IS POSSIBLE

As you may have noticed, I am more interested in the quality of life you can get from real estate investing, not the money you earn. The money just opens you up to really focus on what your calling and higher purpose is.

Through my journey of finding out who I was at a soul level, I was able to become more and more aligned with who I was at the spirit level. Through that search that included psychology, eastern and western numerology, astrology, and akashic records reading, it was easy to be successful because I was in alignment with my soul gifts. Now, I am showing everyone who will listen that Yes! You have a beautiful soul and YES – You're here for a REASON and YES – you have soul gifts too! And you MUST honor them to be successful. And you can learn this all in a week what it took 18 years for me to figure out. If you would like to learn about your unique soul gifts, your soul types, life path and higher calling and purpose in a straightforward way that has your soul saying YES! Then sign up for our email list where we will take you through the process of this easily discovered information step by step. https://bit.ly/SoulPowerBookInvite (case sensitive) or free videos and easy to follow guides YouTube channel at http://bit.ly/SoulPowerOnYoutube (case sensitive).

Resource Guide

The Wealth Building CPA – Ebere Okoye
http://www.thewealthbuildingcpa.com/

Quickbooks Self Employed – http://fbuy.me/jqgcD

Affinity GM – Rental Property Insurance
https://www.nreinsurance.com
(Say affordablerei recommended you for a discount)

Payoff Your Debt App – Helps you pay down your personal debts (which opens you up for investing in rentals). Easy to use and extremely effective.

Legalzoom Prepaid Legal Plans – When you can't afford an attorney at $250 an hour, this will work just as well to get state specific leasing/rental questions answered and protect your assets.

SOFI – In a recent blog post, I used SOFI to get a 15k personal loan over seven years to assist with a renovation. It took four days and I will use them in the future.

Book Recommendations

Tax Free Wealth by Tom Wheelwright – How to Build Massive Wealth by Permanently Lowering Your Taxes

Rich Dad, Poor Dad by Robert Kiyosaki – What the rich teach their kids about money that the poor and middle class do not.

What Wealthy Women Know by Carolyn Hudman – The unspoken rules and everyday investments of the upper–class

Your Limited Liability Company – An Operating Manual by Attorney Anthony Mancuso

Inspecting A House by Rex Cauldwell – For professionals by professionals – takes time to get through, but a lot of good insider information.

The Everything Lease Addendum by Elizabeth Colegrove – especially good for out of state landlords in crafting the perfect lease.

Building Wealth with Inner-city Investing With Al Williamson – How landlords in troubled neighborhoods can increase their cash flow, property values, and quality of tenants.

CPSIA information can be obtained
at www.ICGtesting.com
Printed in the USA
LVHW022303270520
656772LV00018B/2818